Hiram Peck McKnight

Prison Poetry

Hiram Peck McKnight

Prison Poetry

ISBN/EAN: 9783744760539

Printed in Europe, USA, Canada, Australia, Japan

Cover: Foto ©ninafisch / pixelio.de

More available books at **www.hansebooks.com**

PRISON POETRY

BY

H. P. McKNIGHT.

IN LEISURE MOMENTS CAST A LOOK
UPON THE PAGES OF THIS BOOK;
AND IF YOUR THOUGHTS THEY SHOULD ENGAGE,
JUST THINK OF ME WHO WROTE THIS PAGE.
AND IF BY CHANCE, IN YOUR TIME OF LEISURE,
YOU, IN THESE PAGES, SHOULD FIND PLEASURE,
THEN DART YOUR MIND UP TO THIS CELL,
FOR HERE I LIVE IN AN EARTHLY HELL.

DEDICATION.

Go forth, thou little volume,
  I leave thee to thy fate!
To those who read thee faithfully
  Thy leaves I dedicate.

But if your fate should be so sad
  As mine who thee have writ,
I'd be so vexed to think that I
  Had made such a poor " hit."

But if by chance you meet a friend
  Along life's road so dreary,
Just cheer his mind till he is blind,
  And never make him weary.

Teach him the way, the live-long day,
  To lend a helping hand,
And never turn or even spurn
  Those wrecked on life's hard strand.

If chance should be you return to me,
  Along with harvest's golden,
I'll vouch for thee to all who see,
  That thou wilt not embolden.

And now go forth, thou little book,
  I leave thee to thy fate!
To those who read thee faithfully
  Thy leaves I dedicate.

PREFACE.

In the preparation of the verses that fill these pages I have been helped by some of the prisoners of this institution. The donors have been somewhat few, for which I return thanks; but each and every verse is a fair representation of the many phases that the mind of a prisoner passes through, and of his true sentiment. Those that have been donated by my fellow prisoners are accredited to them by either their name or serial number. Some of the verses have been published in our prison "News," but inasmuch as they have reached only an inconsiderable few outside the prison walls, I prepare this litttle volume and hand it to the wide, wide world. My motto, in so doing, is:

May you who enjoy the blessings of liberty and worldly freedom, partake with us of our solitary musings, and enjoy our noblest thoughts and resolutions, as well as for us to enjoy yours; and that you may know that we are not devoid of true, manly, noble principle simply because we are cast—some justly, others unjustly—into prison.

May we exchange greetings with you all—shake—and if by chance I have been fortunate enough to interest you, I am well compensated; but if I have been more fortunate, and given you—even one of you—a line of noble, good thoughts and advice—I say, "May the seed fall on good ground and bring forth good fruit; may it not be wasted upon barren rock." In my work on "Crime and Criminals" many of these verses will appear in the "Appendix."

Very truly yours,

H. P. McKNIGHT,

A. D. 1896.

O. P., Columbus, O., U. S. A.

INTRODUCTION.

True models of poetic art,
Should please the ear and touch the heart;
Stamp on the plastic mind of youth
Due reverence for Eternal Truth.
Paint field and flower in nature's hues,
Give to the world the heart's best news,
Or, lightly tripping o'er the page,
Rejuvenate the blood of age.
The sacred Muse should ne'er descend,
Vice to guild, nor wound a friend.
Heaven gave no man poetic art,
Save to improve the human heart.

You may not find, in coming page,
The ripened wisdom of the age;
Yet you *will* find, untrained by art,
The deathless music of the heart;
And truth shall caress each flaming line,
Inspired by The Tuneful Nine;
No fear of man nor greed of praise
Shall make or mar our tuneful lays;
We simply voice the ripest thought
Of prisoned souls with meaning fraught.
Yours it is to praise or blame
My effort to deserve a name!

CONTENTS.

		PAGE.
Acrostic to Warden and Mrs. Coffin, - By McKnight.		93- 95
Acrostic to Chaplain and Mrs. Winget,	" "	183-185
Acrostic Initial), - - -	" "	167
Acrostic to Capt. J. C. Langenberger, -	" Van Weighs	148
Acrostic to Dr. H. R. Parker, - -	" Harrison,	168
Acrostic to Harry Smith, - - -	" Van Weighs	150
A tribute to Capt. Geo. W. Hess, - -	" " "	143
A Letter From Home, - - -	" 24138,	42
A Memorial Ode, - - -	" Van Weighs	110-111
A Prisoner's Thanksgiving, - -	" McKnight	20-21
A Prisoner's Lamentation, - -	" "	63-64
A Prayer For Justice, - - -	" "	87
A Prison Vision, - - -	" Harrison	95-107
A Query, . - - - -	" Morse	69-70
A Sad Warning, - - -	" Harrison	146-147
An Appreciated Friend, - -	" McKnight	114-115
Be Lenient to the Errant One, -	" Harrison	37
Birthday Musings, - - -	" Van Weighs	88
Coming In and Going Out, - -	" Carr	50-51
Conclusion, - - - -	" McKnight	194
Dreams, - - - -	" "	48
Ella Ree's Revenge, - - -	" "	171-178
Erratic Musings of Unfettered Thought,	" Harrison	25-36
Forget? No, Never! - - -	" McKnight	18
Freedom, - - - -	" "	17
God Bless Them, - - -	" "	18
Guilt's Queries and Truth's Replies, -	" Harrison	41-42
Hope, - - - - -	" Law	39
Hope—Eternity, - - -	" McKnight	21
How To Be Happy In Prison, -	" 22700	23
In Prison, - - - -	" Harrison	24
Influence, - - - -	" Law	36
Judge Not Lest Ye Be Judged, -	" "	72
Kindness, - - - -	" Roth	46
Lines To My Cell, - - -	" McKnight	111-112
Lines To My Wife, - - -	" Harrison	169

CONTENTS.

Love's Victim,	By McKnight	58-63
Last Night In the Dungeon,	" "	38-39
Midnight Musings,	" "	68-69
Mother,	" Overstreet,	19
My Lawyer,	" Gilbert	144-145
My Mother,	" Carr	109-110
My Prison Garden,	" McKnight	11
Our Board of Managers,	" "	65-66
One and a Few,	" 21069	67-68
Out of the Depths	" Harrison	170
Prison Pains,	" "	45
Prisoners,	" McKnight	83
Perfect Peace,	" McKnight	37
Reflections,	" "	43-44
Rhyme and Reason,	" "	11-16
Stray Thoughts,	" "	70-72
Salome's Revenge,	" "	115-142
She Loves Me Yet,	" Harrison	149
Soul Sculpture,	" Doane	51
The Storms of Life,	" Law	57
The Prisoner Released,	" Col. Parsons	44
The Convict's Prayer,	" Harrison	73
The Great "O. P."	" McKnight	49
The Fall of Sodom,	" "	78-80
" " " " Canto Second.	" "	75-80
There Is No Death,	" "	47
The Murderer's Dream,	" "	179-182
The Prisoner's Mother,	" Mrs. Wirick	22
The Reformer,	" Law	43
The Under Dog,	" Barker	45-46
The Phantom Boat,	" Harrison	151-160
To A Departed Idol,	" Van Weighs	91-92
Tribute to Dr. G. A. Tharp.	" "	113
Tribute to the Wolfe Sisters,	" Harrison	89-91
Tribute to the Wolfe Sisters,	" McKnight	81-82
Tribute to Capt. Joseph Smith Acheson,	" Harrison	108
Tribute to Capt. L. H. Wells,	" Van Weighs	66-67
The Mind's the Standard of the Man,	" McKnight	185-190
The Author's Farewell,	" "	192-193
Two Letters,	" Harrison	84-86
Weight and Immortality of Words,	" McKnight	52-53
Which Loved Her Best,	" "	54-57
Wine vs. Water,	" "	74-75
Would They Know,	" Collier	40

PRISON POETRY.

PRELUDE.

If you prefer the sounding line,
Go read some master of the Nine!
Good taste perhaps you will display;
Let others read my simple lay
That gushes from an honest heart
Unawed by fear, unstrained by art.
I ne'er will prostitute my Muse
The rich to praise, nor poor abuse;
But simply sing as best I can
Whate'er may bless my fellow man:
I dare not stain a single page
With outbursts of unreasoning rage.
But if one sorrow I can soothe
Or one his rugged pathway smooth;
One pain relieve, one joy impart,
'Twill ease the burden of a heart
That has known for weary years
No solace save unbidden tears.
Hard is the heart that will refuse
Due merit to the Prison Muse.
May heaven watch the prisoner's weal
And mankind for his sorrow feel!

MY PRISON GARDEN.

In this mind's garden thoughts shall grow,
And in their freshness bud and blow;
Thoughts to which love has beauty lent
And memories sweet of sentiment.
Now, if I cultivate them right good,
They'll furnish me with my mind's food.
My enemies may my corpus hail,
While onward, upward, thoughts will sail
To realms above, where all is peace,
And where the soul may rest with ease.

RHYME AND REASON.

In contravention of the laws of right,
Man's cruel passion and his guilty might,
Has bound me tightly with a galling chain
Of heaped-up malice and unjust disdain!
From front rank lawyer to a felon's cell,
Through perjured villians, not by sin I fell!
By fiat law my body was consigned
To this grim cell for guilty ones designed.
Yet I'm no convict—I have never known
The deep remorse by guilty wretches shown!
I am a martyr—doomed by adverse fate
To brave the billows of malicious hate!
Yet I am free, for Nature's august plan
Makes MIND not *matter* constitute the MAN.

Tho' men may curse me and cast out my name,
Like some vile bauble on the sea of shame;
Brand me as murderer or catiff thief,
Or atheistic infidel—steepid in unbelief;
Foe to all that's pure and good—wretch unfit to live;
Outlaw whom no honest man can even pity give!
Yet my soul will still defy your prison bolts and bars,

And soaring far on eager wings beyond the faintest stars.
Live in a world to you unknown, where only poet soul
Can bask in beauty undefiled by cankering control!
In vain is all your hate and scorn—vain your prison blight;
God loves me, and I feel assured that all will yet be right!
I know one law—a perfect law, by Nature's self designed—
'Tis Heaven's dearest gift to man—The Freedom of the Mind!

If minds and hearts were easy read as faces we can see,
Society would lose its dread and many a prisoner free!
But what, alas! do people care what's in another's brain?
They only seek to hide their share of misery and pain.
Were all compelled to truthful be and show their inner life—
Great heavens! what a jamboree of sin and shame and strife!
    How few would measure half a span if Mind alone we closely scan!
Where is the man on this broad earth, so pure, so good, so true,
That never gave an action birth he dared not bring to view?
The Christ alone was sinless here, none other lives aright;
All human goodness springs from fear of death's approaching night!
There is no soul so white I know but what temptation's power
Its purity can overthrow and all its good deflower!
    Disguise the truth as best we can, he *errs* the most who most is *Man!*

Come, let us take a journey, with cathode rays supplied,
And view the greatest and good in all their pomp and pride!
Examine first the churches, where the godly crew
Teach poor erring mortals what is best to do.
They tell us human nature is *once* and always wrong,
And prove man's deep depravity in sermon or by song.
All natural passion is denounced as deep and deadly sin,
And *truth* and *virtue* painted as graces hard to win.
Heaven, they tell us, is a place with blisses running o'er;
Hell, a lake of torture, where fiery billows roar!
A choice eternal all must make between their birth and death;
It may be made in early life or with expiring breath!
But how this choice must be made each gives a separate plan,
That clearly proves how narrow is the erring mind of Man.

One tells us naught but good pursue, all evil to eschew;
Another swears without God's grace no mortal thus can do;
One bids us work salvation out with trembling and with fear,
Another swears that God's elect should never shed a tear;
One says all must live the life Jesus lived on earth,
Another says it can't be done without a Second Birth!
Some say *work*, others *trust*, others stil say *wait;*
Some deem us mere automatons, saved or lost by *Fate!*
Some, with philanthropic views, declare all must be saved,
Since Christ, the Perfect Offering for *all*, death's horrors braved!
Since Christians never will agree, 'tis best that every man
Should listen to his conscience, and do the best he can!
God ever *has* and *will* do right! In His Eternal Plan
The time will come to set *aright* the numerous wrongs of *Man!*

See yonder's pompous deacon, with diamonds clear and bright;
He looks a model Christian—just turn on him your light.
Great heavens! what a medley of *cant* and sin and shame!
If the half we see was ever told 'twould ruin his good name!
But turn on yonder pastor your strange, mysterious light;
I know he is a real good man, who loves Eternal Right.
Ye holy saints, protect us! *he* too has gone amiss!
When Siren Voice allured him with a seductive kiss!
If half the prayers we utter be not a sounding lie,
It is but little marvel that we are doomed to die!
For each will plead forgiveness for thought or action done,
And *none* by spotless merit eternal bliss hath won.
Then gently judge your fellow, his failings lightly scan;
Like you, he can not corner *all* the brains of man!

See, yonder is our Congress, where wits and fools unite,
To declare by the nation's statute what *is* fundamental right!
They yell of patriotism and the majesty of Law,
And are for once unanimous—their salaries to draw!
Alas! alas! 'tis ever thus within our halls of State;
Sweet Justice is blacklisted—the *dollar* is too great.
Aye, even on judicial bench, where justice should be done,
How scattering are the cases where *Right* the victory won!
Lawyers, judge and jury *exparte* view the case—
An angel would be ruined in the defendant's place!
In vain is protestation, in vain a blameless life;
Some *must be* doomed to prison when prejudice is rife!
Law must keep its servants in stations high and proud,
Tho' every hour should furnish a coffin and a shroud!

The modern Shylock of today, unlike his friend of old,
Demands the pound of quivering flesh and *all* his victim's gold;
Nor feels content until he sees his victim's hated face
Behind a wall of rock and steel in garments of disgrace.
Then he will raise his dainty hands and loud applaud the law
That *can* protect such beings, who live without a flaw.
He has no pity for the weak, who thro' temptation fall,
But freely spends his *time* and *means* the guileless to enthrall.
He heaps *his* mighty wrath and scorn on every evil done,
And speaks in tones of pure disgust of poverty's pale son.
But if you bid him look within and study his own heart,
He has a task herculean—'tis such a *tiny* part!
And as for Mind—ye angels! in fair creation's plan
'Twas given to his victim, and left him *half a man!*

The modern Clytemnestra no dagger needs to use;
She slays her agememnon within your *legal* pews,
Since judges now are willing to sunder marriage ties,
And juries are so truculent when blushing beauty lies.
Or if she be a *Helen*, and Paris suits her taste,
She hastes without compunction to lay her honor waste.
"Society" allows her to have "a special friend,"
And a husband is *so* handy her good name to defend!
But alas! Aspasia *no mercy* need expect;
Her Pericles *lionized*, but none *her* worth detect!
And as for poor Thargelia *none* will take *her* part;
She lives a social outcast, with broken, bleeding heart;
But each base seducer, in our social plan,
Makes poor, trusting woman bear the sins of *Man!*

Many men are now misjudged, and meet an awful fate,
Whose innocence is published, but alas, it is too late!
Many, too, are breathing freedom's precious air
Whose vile conduct merits prison dress and fare.
Only *little* rascals in your prisons *die*,
While *stupendous* villians liberty can buy!
Each one strives with fervor his neighbor to outshine,
And he who has the most of gold is reckoned half divine.
You scatter dark temptations around the poor man's path,
And when he falls you pour on him *all* your vicious wrath.
Poverty in public lives all her deeds are seen;
Wealth can build a castle her *wickedness* to screen.
Yet many a noble woman and kingly man is found
As toilers in your factories or tillers of the ground!

If cathode rays were freely used to bring to human sight
The dirty methods villians use to *down* Eternal Right,
Many men would be set free and others take their place
Who now can roll in luxury and laugh at their disgrace.
A judge and jury now can sit and *hang* a man at will,
But they say 'tis open *murder* if but *one* dares kill!
Take a ring of brass and plate it o'er with gold,
And 'tis only *business* when the fraud is sold!
Adulterate both food and drink, deal in deadly pills;
Law will aid your *robbery* and collect your bills!
Give to your profession but a sounding name,
Then cut up the devil without fear or shame.
Be sure to call it *business* whatever you may do,
And if you have sufficient *gall* that will pull you through.

Now throughout this prison rays cathodal dart,
And read the hidden secrets of each convict heart.
Some have wrought vile deeds, and wrought them o'er and o'er,
That surely proves them rotten to their inmost core.
And here are wretched fiends, who with consumate art,
Ravish every instinct of the human heart.
Some men of wit and letters, cultured and refined,
Others moral lepers, with heart and conscience blind.
From drawing room and brothel, farm and city slum,
Some by acts of justice, some through perjury come;
The innocent and guilty, callow youth and age,
All can be imprisoned in this Christian age!
But they who seek for liberty no innocence must plead—
Gold, and plenty of it, will be all they need.

Some young souls are making, for a stated time,
This, their maiden effort, on the sea of crime.
Oh, Christians, teach them early what to me is plain;
Crime ever *has* and ever *will* result in lasting pain.
Do not be *too* lenient, nor *too* soon forgive,
Lest all *vice* should flourish and no *virtue* live.
Society demands it, the *guilty* should atone—
But take care you punish those, and those *alone!*
Keep them in your prisons till by *virtue* shown
They will know what *is* and what is *not* their own.
But let all be careful lest by *word* or *act*
Those who should *reform* them from their *good* subtract.
Rule them wisely, gently—by some *humane* plan,
All their faults to conquer as best becomes a MAN.

When your work is finished and their habits changed,
Give them honest labor, by the State arranged;
Show them honest labor *can* a living gain,
While the *social outcast* harvests *want* and *shame!*
Treat them fairly, kindly; teach them all the true
Will be friendly with them while *the right* they do.
Both principle and policy declare this course is wise;
Then why longer act the fool and wisdom's voice despise?
Crime never *can* nor *will* decrease until in *Wisdom's School*
Men learn the noted lesson, "Right *through* Law should Rule."
All tried plans are failures, this none dares deny;
Now give *Common Sense* a show and failure dare defy.
Do *this*, and lash and pistol, now your sole defense,
Shall give place to Reason and plain Common Sense!

Courts are far too careless when they give men life
For offense unnoticed save in time of strife.
Naught but some poor chicken or a ham he stole—
Shall the devil purchase at such price a soul?
If such petty crimes as this deserve such prison fare,
Come now, honest reader, what is *your* just share?
Was that old Greek right, who, tho' a man of sense,
Could meet out death to all for each small offense?
Apply his heartless rule, and can you truly say
Any man or woman would be left to slay?
Man is only mortal, and to sin is prone;
Never cure another's faults till you quit your own.
Many are convicted by the *press* at large;
The Public Mind is rarely Heaven's peculiar charge.

Bring the judge and jury who declared my fate
For the shining dollars furnished them by hate,
And their guilty conscience by my own arrange,
And then tell me frankly if my fate should change!
Yet I had sooner die behind these bars of steel
Than to have a heart of stone that *could* not feel!
I know such human tigers, who fatten on distress,
Never *can* and *never* will enjoy one hour of rest!
Until all hate and malice, all greed and other sin
Is burned by awful torture to leave them pure within!
God *will* forgive each penitent whate'er his sin may be,
Whose heart is overflowing with *love* for bond and free.
Oh listen! brothers, listen—'tis Jehovah's plan—
And a *time is fixed* to right the wrongs of Man.

FREEDOM.

How sweet thou art, O freedom,
  To every human heart—
Man's privilege most sacred,
  His being's noblest part.
Thou priceless, great possession,
  Without thee life were done!
Its sun gone down forever,
  For thou and life are one.

How dear thou art, O freedom—
  Our birthright here below!
Chief blessing of all blessings
  Kind heaven doth bestow.
Deprived by dark misfortune
  Of every other joy,
Naught while thou still remainest
  Can happiness destroy.

But thou, O prison penance,
  Dark shadow by life's board!
Of all that men hold mournful
  Thou art the fullest stored.
There's naught on earth worth having
  If 't must be shared with thee—
O happy, holy freedom!
  O heaven, set me free.

GOD BLESS THEM!

God bless the mothers of this land!
   They are so good and true;
And all the sisters of their band,
   They are so noble, too.
If we don't treat them with respect.
   And court their wholesome 'fluence.
Our morals will not be correct,
   And we will suffer hence.

If women are not treated with respect, and made to exercise an influence over the social world, the standard of private virtue and public opinion will be lowered, and the morals of men will suffer.

FORGET? NO, NEVER!

There are things we'll not remember,
   And much will be forgot,
As in the bleak December
   When our coffee was not hot;
When the butter was much younger,
   When the bread was sour and dry;
When are felt the pangs of hunger,
   With regrets and many a sigh.
How the memory used to vex us
   As 'twould o'er our senses steal;
How we wished they might "annex" us,
   So we'd get one good square meal.
Other things may be forgot
   In this busy, hustling age,
But one thing we ne'er can blot
   From off our memory's page,
That we never can forget
   In a hundred months of Junes;
It will long our memories fret—
   Those prunes—those rotten, wormy prunes.

MOTHER.

BY OVERSTREET.

Who is it, in this life so drear,
  That pines for the wandering boy,
And ever ready with words of cheer
  To turn sad thoughts to joy?
    Mother.

Who is it, when all others do forsake
  And leave us to our grief,
That will for long hours lie awake
  And pray for our relief?
    Mother.

Who is it, when the world laughs on
  And gives our sighs no thought,
That thinks of the boy who looks upon
  This life that's come to naught?
    Mother.

Who is it, when from prison freed—
  The boy goes forth so sadly—
That receives him in his hour of need
  With tears of joy—yea, gladly?
    Mother.

Who is it, when the end has come,
  Looks fondly on her child,
And prays to God for a happy home
  For the boy that's been so wild?
    Mother.

A Prisoner's Thanksgiving.

What if the gold of the corn lands
  Is faded to somber grey?
And what if the down of the thistle
  Is ripened and scattered away?
There's a crowning golden harvest,
  There's turkey the heart to cheer,
There's a basket from home with plenty of "pone,"
  Tho' 'tis bathed in a mother's tear.

What 'f our friends are far from us
  And they know not where we are?
What if those who are dearest
  Live ever away so far?
There's room for us by th' fireside,
  Where in childhood days we'd play;
'Tis comfort to think, tho' we stand on the brink,
  That we will be there some day.

What if our hearts are lonely
  As we toil in our enemy's hand?
What if our sad looks betray us
  As we take a true manly stand?
There's a coming golden harvest,
  There's a time when we all 'll meet,
When prison locks and iron bars
  Will fail to ther pris'n'r keep.

What care we for the pang at heart?
  'Twill all be gone some day;
And then tho' our enemies 'ld crush us,
They'll be scattered far away.
  Tho' this is a sad Thanksgiving,
A better one's coming our way,
  When we'll all be home to share in the "pone"
And hear our angeled sister pray.

What if the gold of the corn lands
  Is faded to somber grey?
And what if the down of the thistle
  Is ripened and scattered away?

Away to the east in a far off land
  There's turkey the heart to cheer,
Where the dear ones are partaking
  And thinking of one that's here:
There's father and mother and sister and brother, all so far away,
  There's a blessed time a-coming—
The prisoner's Thanksgiving day.

HOPE---ETERNITY.

The heart bowed down with silent grief,
  Despair its portals soon assails.
Oh! let such moments be but brief
  When spirit lost o'er man prevails;
Think not of friend who, false, betrayed,
  Nor sweetheart's change, nor colder wife—
Recall those oaths when passion prayed
  For vengeance and for foeman's life.

We pass dear friends but once this way;
  Our judge, accusers and our foe,
If false to God and man they play,
  Not thou, but they, shall suffer woe.
All stay is short; the longest span
  Counts less than raindrops in the sea.
Arouse thee, then, despairing man,
  And hail with hope—Eternity!

Glows in thy cell a fragrant bloom,
  Plucked from thy guardian angel's wreath.
Do thou but nurture it with prayer
  And water it with tears of faith,
To humble hearts its petals ope,
  Revealing bliss to streaming eye—
Immortal blooms this rose of hope,
  God's flower of life—Eternity.

THE PRISONER'S MOTHER.

BY MRS. S. E. WIRICK.

To be a prisoner's mother
  Is to feel a piercing dart
That sets the mind a-whirling
  And almost cleaves the heart.

To be a prisoner's mother
  Is, upon a holiday,
To visit him in prison,
  Then part and go away.

To be a prisoner's mother
  'Tis, inside the lonely wall,
To say, " Farewell, my darling "—
  Oh, I almost faint and fall.

No resting place but heaven,
  No happy morn that dawns;
Our home so drear and lonely
  Because our boy is gone.

An empty bed, a missing plate,
  A grief that inward burns;
No balm on earth to heal our hearts
  Until our boy returns.

" Honor and shame from no condition rise:
  Act well your part, there all the honor lies."

HOW TO BE HAPPY IN PRISON.

BY NO. 22700.

Do what is right, and day by day
Teach yourself that work is play
Of brain and muscle, rightly used—
And hurtful only when abused;
Deep interest take in all you do;
'Twill others please, as well as you.

Relieve a fellow prisoner's need;
Righteous counsel always heed;
Be not suspicious or unjust—
Few men betray a perfect trust;
He trusts the most whose heart is pure,
And generous thought will malice cure.

Brood not o'er the ills of life;
Give no cause for needless strife;
Tomb the past with all its sin;
Purify yourself within;
Rear your standard, be a MAN,
And do whatever good you can.

Some, perhaps, will misconstrue
All you say and all you do,
But when conscience is at rest
Happiness will fill the breast—
'Twill be a sweet red-letter day
When we all shall act that way.

IN PRISON.

BY HARRISON.

That which the world miscals a jail
   A private closet is to me;
Whilst a good conscience is my bail,
   And innocence my liberty:
Locks, bars and solitude together met
Make me no prisoner, but an anchoret.

I, whilst I wisht to be retired,
   Into this private room was turned,
As if their wisdoms had conspired
   The salamander should be burned;
Or, like those sophists that would drown a fish.
I am constrained to suffer what I wish.

These manacles upon my arm
   I as my mistress' favors wear;
And for to keep my ankles warm
   I have some iron shackles there:
These walls are but my garrison; this cell,
Which men call jail, doth prove my citadel.

I'm in the cabinet lockt up,
   Like some high-prized margarite,
Or, like the Great Mogul or Pope,
   Am cloistered up from public sight:
Retiredness is a piece of majesty,
And thus, proud Sultan, I'm as great as thee.

Erratic Musings of Unfettered Thought

[BY GEO. W. H. HARRISON.]

Is living thought, proud condor of the mind,
By walls of rock and iron bars confined,
Innate divinity by human courts enslaved,
And right eternal by a dust-worm braved?
Think you the spirit's rapid flight to mar
With dungeon torture and by iron bar?
Can rock-ribbed walls and bars of steel
Deprive man of the power to feel?
Can you the stream of Lethe roll
In maddening torrents o'er the soul,
Pluck from my brow love's garland fair
And brand me " Victim of despair?"
No! weakling son of vengeful fate,
God grants to none a power so great.
My body is your lawful prey,
Poor lump of spirit-crumbling clay;
Seize, chain and manacle each part,
Aye, even starve my bleeding heart,
But know that for Creative Thought
All fetters by one's self is wrought.
Mind, glorious Mind—Jehovah's sleepless breath,
Can know no bondage and can feel no death.
In yon fair regions of unreached repose
Eternal Beauty's flower-chalice glows,
Filled to the brim with satisfying wine,
Ambrosial nectar of the Tuneful Nine.
My muse can reach it on external wings
And drink till all the heart within me sings!
I scale the lofty heights, by virtue shown,
And from Eternal Wisdom seek my own.
There, far above the struggling world of fate,
I greet true freedom and am wisely great.
'Tis mine in bright elysian fields to roam,
Pluck jeweled treasure from the sleeping gnome;
Bid ocean deeps their mysteries reveal,
Or, soaring far above the world of space,
Gain raptured visions of the Holy Place;
Admire and measure every glittering throne,

Count heavenly treasure as my own,
Make august angels bow beneath my rod,
And even dare to mould the mind of God;
O radiant fields of pure, untrammeled Thought,
With what sweet incense are thy zephyrs fraught;
How clear the view, from thy exalted height,
Of human errors and unerring right;
'Tis thou alone my laboring Muse can teach
The perfect measure of her powers to reach;
She cons these fragments of a Truth sublime,
And art stands ready with appropriate rhyme
To trim each sentence and each word to place
In melting numbers of seductive grace;
Since first Jehovah, bending low to earth,
Breathed in man's nostrils an eternal birth.
The rain drop falling, from the heavy cloud,
In waiting dust, finds ready shroud,
And there commingling fills each separate cell,
Yet still remains as pure as when it fell:
To man appearing but a dampened clod,
'Tis chambered favor of a gracious God;
And serves his purpose till He calls above
This liquid semblance of Immortal Love,
There *not* to perish, but return again
To deck the forest and adorn the plain;
All nature feels its fructifying power
In laughing streamlets and in nodding flower;
The rain drop typifies the Pure Indwelling God,
That permeates our being, to animate a clod;
Give birth to all emotion, consistent with His plan,
And with unmeasured tenderness weep the fall of man.
From every nodding flower, from every whispering breeze
From mountain's lofty height, from towering trees,
From softly twinkling star, from lightning's giddy flash,
From the softest twitter of a bird and thunder's awful crash.
From hills the ants may call their own,
From crested elders 'round their throne,
From babbling brook, from storm-lashed wave,
From nature smiling, nature grave,
From earth and air, from sky and sea,
There comes the self same voice to me,
Like softest note of cooing dove,
And sweetly whispers, "GOD IS LOVE."

All nature is obedient to heaven's august plan,
And none will dare rebellion, save ever-erring man.
He, of a dual nature—purity and lust—
Defies his Great Creator and thus betrays his trust.
Thrones within his being the hydra-headed sin,
All his joy to murder and create *hell within;*
Self-conscienceness completes the triple blow
While memories of happier years augments his hapless woe.
Whatever then of pleasure his wounded spirit knows
From the fountain of bitter repentence it onward, onward flows.
His own environment, be it either fair or fell,
Must *now* embower his heaven, or will create his hell.
Contentment, peace, or pleasure he must create anew
By sowing seeds of virtue where vice so lately grew.
He learns he must not do whatever man can do,
But recognize the limits of the just and true.
Law is his *Alma mater*, the measure of his right,
The barrier Jehovah set to curb irreverent flight;
He has the truest liberty who recognizes law;
'Tis made to shield his virtues and on his vices war;
He who denies humanity lives for himself alone
All history to hush, all culture to disown;
And quickly he relapses into a barbarous state,
Where only force and prowess can make the unit great.
None so lost to *virtue*, none so devoid of art,
As he who fails to capture *the empire of a heart;*
He who knows not sympathy feels no fellow's woe,
Will never feel the rapture of happiness below;
God planted seeds of pity in every human breast,
And he who loses most of woe secures most of rest;
Love is man's *all*, his conqueror, his cordial and wine,
The measure of his inner life that stamps him as divine.
How circumscribed the circle God allots to man,
His home is but an acre, his life is but a span;
And yet within that circle his influence is so great
He wakes the cooing notes of *love* or feeds the fires of hate;
His influence is potential within a circle small,
But beyond the limit of the same he does no good at all;
All thought, all power with which our being teems,
Is action predicated on events or on dreams.
All we have seen or heard, all we now can feel,
Leaves an imprint on the heart that the future must reveal;
The vain are truly lonely, they long to be admired,

One wishes to be understood, another well attired,
This hushed by useless longings or fashion's changing art.
That sweetest of all poems, *the music of the heart.*
But he who solves life's mystery is never quite alone.
All ages is his playground and solitude his throne;
He walks in subtle converse with all the mighty dead,
Gathering priceless jewels their wit or wisdom bred.
The watchtowers of his thought o'erlooks the struggling mass,
While events both past and present before his vision pass.
He sees the weary captive tugging at his chain;
The weather-beaten sailor plough the raging main;
The swarthy burden bearer in forest, mine and field;
The merchant's soiled ledgers, the soldier's brazen shield;
The child with glittering toy, the maiden at her glass;
The ruler of an empire, the leader of the mass;
The student in his study, the priest on bended knee;
The teacher with his ferrule, the aged human tree,
All fondly dream of freedom, yet all beneath the ban,
Each in a separate prison presided o'er by *man ;*
Sees *nature* and *morality* are ever waging war.
The first as god of freedom, the latter lord of law.
Sees culture raise her barriers between polite and rude,
And hears *Religion* thunder, "Cover up the nude!"
Knows man in every station to be a willing slave,
The football of his passion, the dupe of every knave.
Yet hears him boast his freedom, laud his reasoning power;
Rule all he can with iron hand, and *finite* judgment shower;
Sees all the devious, hidden paths by sinful mortals trod
Where *human* law and custom dare ostracise a god;
Yet knows a germ of goodness, deep in the human breast,
Is living in the worst of men however much depressed.
Knows life is but the unit of God's Eternal Plan,
And learns to *pity*, not to blame, poor ever-erring man!
In each created atom sees faultless beauty glow
And God's Eternal purpose in onward sequence flow.
Views all souls as living harps, whose seeming dissonance
Is but apparent and not real; and believes, perchance,
God will mend each shattered chord, tune the quivering lyre,
And from out each soul shall bring a music sweeter, higher
Than earthly ears have ever heard or earthly lips essayed;
Such music as the ransomed sing in innocence arrayed;
While all the universe entranced shall wondering inquire:
"Is this the fruitage of *His* woe? Is this his soul's desire?

Is this the harp so late unstrung? Is this poor fallen man?
Ah! can it be that all was wrought obedient to God's plan?

Nature will o'er matter bear imperial sway,
And all not immortal must in time decay;
Man's tenement is mortal, but himself divine;
Which should he most cherish, the jewel or its shrine?
Yet when vice allures him with seductive ray,
Gives he not to passion undisputed sway?
Dreams he not of beauty who, with open arms,
Calls for lust to enter and revel 'mid her charms?
Is his eye not captive? Do not his senses thrill?
What is left the tempted one save his feeble will?
If that will prove recreant to Jehovah's trust,
Pays he not the penalty in self-consuming lust?
Must his spirit suffer through unending years
For the shame he purchased with agonizing tears?
Life is but a shoe-broom, Nature is God's book
And he's the aptest scholar who all her laws can brook!
If love of right was constant man could well defy
All of sin's allurements and unspotted die!
One such man has lived who, with a faith sublime,
Crucified the temple where he dwelt in time,
And entered heaven victorious without the aid of grace,
The marvel of all centuries, the Savior of the race;
But had His will but weakened, Jesus, too, had fell,
And man without Redemption sank tottering into hell:
All would be good did not true goodness claim
Such earnest noble effort from a will so tame;
Crime is but a sequence of misguided will
Inherent moral defect and *surrounding* ill.
Man's innate love of beauty and his dread of pain,
His ever raging thirst for power and his greed for gain
Alternately do sway him with resistless power,
The spotless blossoms of the soul, until he only yearns
For the ever hideous lust that blackens as it burns.
Guilt comes not, thundering on the wings of time,
With vice-distorted feature and the leer of crime,
But like enchanting vision from a pagan dream,
Or softly echoed cadence of a whispering stream,
She steals upon us gently, with ever-changing art,
And usurps an empire—the waiting human heart!
Her outward form is beauty, her voice with Passion tense,

She only craves the privilege to gratify each sense:
All apparent pleasures 'round her path are spread,
But, alas! you seize the flower to find its fragrance fled;
But still pursuing, row with bated breath,
You clasp her to your bosom and—embrace a death!
Then, conscience stricken, you the wreck survey,
And with shuddering horrow—humbly kneel to pray:
While the pitying angels on their pinions bear
The ever sacred burden of repentant prayer,
And almighty love descending reasserts control,
And mercy in the guise of grace has won a human *soul;*
But contrast a moment, with this heavenly plan,
The awful brutal conduct of exacting MAN.
See yon martial champion riding on the flood
Of a frightful carnage and a sea of blood;
His path is strewn with many a ghastly sight,
Dead and dismembered bodies and defenseless fright!
Yet all the people with a loud acclaim
Pronounce *him* " *Hero*," and accord him Fame!
True, he butchers thousands in a cruel war,
Yet you deem him *guiltless*, he obeyed *your* law.
But if your angered brother slay a single man,
Him you brand a " Murderer," worthy of your ban;
And with zeal unbounded you wage relentless war
Until he falls, a victim to rage-created law.
As if a useless *murderer*, sanctioned by the state,
Was less the fruitage of revenge than one new-born of hate;
Perchance in some fair aiden, some far distant sphere
Your poor hapless victim these just words may hear:
"'Thou art now forgiven, poor misguided son!
" Tho' tranced with dire passion thou hast slain but one.
" Thou hast made atonement, breathed a fiery breath
" Of a deep repentance and an awful death!
" Place on him the raiment—whiter far than snow,
" And teach his untried lips to sing the song the angels know.
" But as to yonder soldier who for the bauble fame
" Led unbattled thousands without fear or shame;
" And with banners flying to the bugle's chime
" Hurled obedient legions into conscious crime—
" All the tears he showed, *all* the blood he shed,
" Now in molten fire shall circle 'round his head,
" And all shall learn the lesson, that horror-breeding war
" Will *never* meet the sanction of Jehovah's law!"

This is no fancy picture, nor idle dream of youth,
But, if I know the laws of God, it is the solemn truth.

Behold a homeless wanderer, poor and thinly clad,
To biting cold a victim, with hunger almost mad,
Entering yonder mansion, dares to boldly steal
What none should e'er deny a dog--the pittance of a meal!
See the greedy sleuth-hounds of the outraged law
Wage against this robber an unrelenting war;
While *Christian* judge and jury, with ready wit, declare
His crime an awful outrage, that merits prison fare!
But he who rears his costly domes
O'er wreck and ruin of human homes,
Plants in the breast a raging thirst
And leaves his victims doubly cursed,
Can roll in luxury, loll in pride
And, with *the law*, his gain divide!
Tho' every dime he pays the state
A thousand cost in wakened hate!

A simple youth by passion lured,
And of but little wisdom steward,
Meets with a maid of witching grace
And dalliance ends in dire disgrace!
In prison stripes you teach the fool
That he must *love* by *human* rule!
Yet you rear great, costly piles
Where soiled doves may ply their wiles
And lead to an unhallowed bed
The lustful brute you lately wed.
If passion will assert her power
None shall dare a maid deflower
Unless so *licensed* by the state
In wedlock's bonds his lust to sate!
And, if marriage prove a bane,
Divorce, for cash, will ease his pain!
Then to your haunts of sin he hies
And laws of God and man defies
By casting, in a barren sea,
The germ of *life* that is to be!
'Tis true this evil you decry—
And raise your taxes mountain high!
As if the more the state shall gain

The less will virtue feel the strain!—
You legalize *divorce* and *fraud*,
And each *successful* scoundrel laud,
Unmindful tho' he gain his wealth
By open plunder or by stealth.
In vain his hapless victims cry,
His *gold* can legal silence buy!
But if through stress of penury's strife
One makes a shipwreck of his life,
You prisons build and place within
This fruitage of a law-made sin,
To linger till the cowering slave
Shall fill—unwept—a pauper's grave.
And scarce a line of obscure print
At this dark tragedy will hint;
But if your millioned puppy dies
What wailings rend the astonished skies!
What sabled hue and lengthened train
Attest your deep regret and pain!
How yon cathedral's vaulted arch
Will echo with his funeral march;
What flowers will deck his costly tomb;
What tapers rob the grave of gloom;
While columns, nay, whole papers tell
How *great* a man to-day has fell.
Deluded mortals! raise your eyes
To yon fair regions of the skies,
Where *justice* sits, each cause to try
Beneath Omniscience's searching eye;
Your "*convict*," on low bended knee,
Pleads "guilty"—and they set him free;
And angels crown, with loud acclaim,
The man you deemed a living shame!
Your *Crœsus*, with uplifted eye,
(Still conscious of his station high)
Deigns to repeat, with growing stress,
How from defeat he wrung success;
Tells, with a proudly swelling heart,
Of millions spent on sculptured art;
And millions more on lordly hall,
The eye and heart of man to thrall;
Tells how a church and college new
From *his* donation quickly grew;

Tells how in cushioned pew he knelt
And begged God other hearts to melt,
Until each child of man should be,
Like his dear self, from error free;
All this they hear your idol tell
And cast him headlong into hell!
While heaven bows her head with awe
In sanction of Jehovah's law.

What mighty solons fill your halls of state!
 Poor gibbering parrots with an empty pate,
Who deem all prisons of but little use
Not founded on starvation and abuse.
They lock poor pris'ners in a loathsome cell,
While lash and pistol drives them on to hell;
They crush his manhood and his soul debase,
Blot out ambition and his name disgrace,
Yet wonder greatly that such humane plan
Makes not an angel of each convict man.
These truthful samples of your legal page
Condemn your judgment and disgrace your age—
Too oft repeated, who will dare to say
To what dark horrors they may pave the way?
Pause! ere the records that now strew your path
Invite the vengeance of Jehovah's wrath;
Relearn the lesson early taught mankind,
" To God give reverence and to man be kind."
Be this your motto, and each setting sun
Will kiss the feature of a work begun;
Time cannot tarnish and no heart can blame
Your noble effort to deserve a name;
Heaven will applaud you, and the smile
Of happiness the hours beguile,
Why pay such homage to mere human laws?
Dread you man's censure or admire applause?
Are you forgetful that the crown of fame
Is purchased torture and expiring shame?
Think you man's plaudits or his causeless hate
Can either ope or close the pearly gate?
Whoever placed in man implicit trust,
Nor saw his idol, soon or late, in dust?
Why thus pursue an ever fading wraith?
'T is God, and God alone, deserves your faith.

Survey all things with comprehensive view,
Admire all beauty and enthrone the true;
Know every mortal, tho' a separate soul,
Is but a fragment of the mighty whole
That fills a niche in God's eternal plan,
All for the welfare of ungrateful man;
Learn that in many a loathsome cell
A prisoned genius or a saint may dwell,
Whose power, developed by an act of love,
May lead a million to the Courts above.
Shall it be yours to touch that vibrant chord
And share the honor of the great reward?
What heaven endorses that alone can stand;
All else is stubble, built on shifting sand,
That shall vanish 'mid the fire and flood
Like tiny snowflakes in a sea of blood.
Oh, could my Muse, by some exalted flight,
Portray her knowledge of Eternal Right—
Breathe in soft accents to the listening ear
The melting music which my soul can hear,
Some would declare my reason half dethroned
Before my fancy to such heights had flown;
Yet could such see as I have seen the scroll
Where God has written " Destiny of Soul,"
They much would wonder how my Muse
Could dare suppress such glorious news.
What pen can picture or what brush can paint
The endless rapture of a raptured saint?
Words are too feeble; they but tell in part
The truthful language of a human heart;
But, Oh, when spirit from its cumbering clay
Shall rise triumphant to the realms of day,
What strains seraphic from our lips shall break
Till all creation shall to bliss awake!
O bliss supernal! when our lips shall meet—
The lips long buried—and our souls shall greet
The loved and cherished of those earlier years.
Ere pain had turned each quivering chord to tears,
And life was smiling in her morning hours
And love was conscious of her magic powers.
Oh, sweet reunion on the crystal strand!
When we shall fondly clasp the waiting hand
Of buried jewels distance hides from view,

And all the plighted vows of life renew,
Then shall we learn the truthfulness of love,
When hearts like ours, renewed in youth, above
All passion and the cloying cares of earth
Shall wake to rapture with a Second Birth!

O hearts estranged, forgive and be forgiven!
Your cruel coldness has already driven
The angel sweetness from your speaking eye,
And suffered everything, save pride, to die.
O cradle, in the lap of everlasting sleep
The dark, fierce passions that now rudely sweep
The sounding chambers of the suffering soul,
Where Hate's tumultuous torrents hourly roll,
And blacken what was once so white and fair,
When spotless Innocence was centered there!
Oh, keep no kisses for my cold, dead brow
I am so lonely—let me feel them now.
When dreamless sleep is mine I never more can need
The tenderness for which tonight I plead;
My wayworn spirit and my thorn-pierced feet
The piteous pleadings of my lips repeat.
Oh, shall I plead and plead with you in vain
To bring love's sunlight to my soul again?
Shall acts repented, bred of undue haste,
Lay all my stock of future pleasures waste?
Bid me to draw a servile, galling chain,
Nor wish to murmur, nor murmur to complain?
Will you deprive my hungry soul of love,
Nor leave one spark of happiness above?
Oh, what base deed has these my fingers wrought
To wake a malice with each vengeance fraught?
If I have sinned and disobeyed your laws,
Discarded fashion and despised applause,
Have I not suffered all a man can know,
And drank the bitterest dregs of human woe?
Think you my proud and haughty soul to cower
With scorpion lashes of tempestuous power?
Go scourge the ocean with puny lash,
Or raze a mountain with a feather's crash!
Why thus torment my swift declining age
With useless torture of unreasoning rage?
'T were best to sound the caverns of my soul

And learn the being whom you dare control!
'T will teach you wisdom in a single hour
And rob your malice of its wasting power!
For heaven has writ upon each poet soul
"DEAL GENTLY WITH HIM AND HIS ALL CONTROL."

INFLUENCE.

BY SAM LAW.

When e'er a noble deed is wrought,
When e'er is spoke a noble thought,
    Our hearts, in glad surprise,
    To higher levels rise.

The sleeping purpose wakes in us,
Arousing power or genius,
    And from their exercise
    Is born good enterprise.

Honor to those whose words or deeds
Thus help us in our prison needs,
    And by their overflow
    Raise us from what is low.

PERFECT PEACE.

["Thou wilt keep him in perfect peace."—Isaiah xxvi, 3.]

Peace, perfect peace, in this dark world of sin,
The blood of Jesus whispers peace within;
Peace, perfect peace, for loved ones far away;
In Jesus' keeping we are safe and they.
Peace, perfect peace, with sorrows surging 'round,
On Jesus' bosom naught but calm is found;
Peace, perfect peace, our future all unknown;
Jesus we know, and He is on the throne.
Peace, perfect peace, death shadowing us and ours;
Jesus has vanquished death and all its powers.
It is enough, earth's struggles soon shall cease,
And Jesus calls to Heaven's own perfect peace.

BE LENIENT TO THE ERRANT ONE.

BY GEO. W. H. HARRISON.

Like phantoms wierd of troubled dream,
In they come—a ceaseless stream—
The callow youth, the aged sire,
To reap the fruit of Satan's hire.

With pallid brow and rueful face
They view their garments of disgrace,
And oft in eyes unused to weep
Unbidden tears will slowly creep.

Be lenient with the blighted crowd;
Some come, perhaps, to greet a shroud;
Some, perhaps, will go outside
And yet become a nation's pride.

If by kindness you reclaim
A single soul from crime and shame,
God will reward the noble deed
And aid you in the hour of need.

LAST NIGHT IN THE DUNGEON.

The darkness of hades and a vile, deathly smell
  Is all that I feel stealing over my senses.
As lingering alone in this cold dungeon cell,
  Shut away from the world, where hearts' blood condenses,
  I feel 't is too much for slight, trivial offenses.

Shut away from the dear ones, the loved ones on earth,
  I suffer the tortures that no man can tell
Till he 's taken away from fireside and hearth
  And sees the sad visions of a dungeon cell
  Then he feels that vile man can create a real hell.

As I sit here alone, my head throbbing and aching,
  And listen to hear if the keeper is near,
My thoughts they roam back to little ones taking
  Caresses so sweet from a mother so dear—
  Then I 'm prompted to ask, "Do they think of me here?"

But when in my heart I feel a slight flutter,
  I know there is sympathy somewhere about;
I then to myself do silently mutter,
  "They have love for me still, and there is no doubt;"
  Aye, love for me still, and this I 've found out.

Then, down on the damp and cold stony floor,
  Without either pillow, or blanket, or gown,
I stretch my weak body right close to the door,
  And there, in sweet sleep, my vision to drown—
  Then, when I awake, I 'm not so cast down.

There is nothing so sweet and perfectly soothing
  To one who is placed in a cold dungeon cell,
As the thought that yet there are dear ones a-wooing
  The one who 's imprisoned in a dark, dreary dell—
  I muttered, while sleeping, "'T is well, ah, 't is well."

Then, when I awoke and proceeded to think,
  Cold, stiffened and hungry, with tongue parched from thirst,
I seek but in vain for food and for drink,
  But bread and poor water, the same as at first
  Aye, dry bread and bad water, the same as at first.

Then my heart sank within me, so weak and so pale,
  As I gazed on the keeper of dungeon and jail
And begged for a drink of pure Adams' ale,
  As he held in his hand a full water pail-
  But the answer came back, " Your plea it must fail."

Then, giving it up in pure desperation,
  I try to surpass the curse of damnation
That springs to my lips ere I can but control
  The blood that is boiled by such torturing droll—
  Then I whisper, " Be still! Some one loves this poor soul."

Then, staid by the love of those dear ones at home,
  I steady myself and go swimming along;
I brave the hard life of a dark dungeon cell
  And I come out victorious, all perfect and well—
  Then I meet them again and go home there to dwell.
       'T is well! Ah, 't is well!

HOPE.

BY SAM LAW.

The world may change from old to new,—
  From new to old again,—
Yet Hope and Heaven, forever true,
  Within man's heart remain.
The dreams that bless the weary soul,
  The struggle of the strong,
Are steps toward some happy goal,
The story of Hope's song.

WOULD THEY KNOW?

BY 25700.

If, amid these prison shadows,
　These pale lips should breathe their last,
Would my friends regret the summons,
　And forgive my guilty past?

Would they know the dire temptations
　I had met and nobly braved
Ere the tears in guilty passion
　My pale cheeks in torrents laved?

Would they know how oft and earnest
　I had plead before the throne
For the place my crime made vacant
　In the bosom of my own?

Would these hours of retribution
　Prove sufficient for my sin?
Would the gates of glory open
　To let this weary wanderer in?

Hear, Oh, hear! From yonder heaven
　Speaks the Lamb once crucified:
"Look up, sad one; never falter;
　For such sinners once I died."

GUILT'S QUERIES AND TRUTH'S REPLIES.

BY HARRISON.

GUILT.

Will the fountain of life, now bathed in tears,
Ebb and flow ten weary years?
Will the soul escape the horrible blight
That stalks in prison's gruesome night?

TRUTH.

Trust, weary one, alone in ME;
Living or dead, thou shalt be free
From prison blight and sin's alarms,
While closely nestling in my arms.

GUILT.

Will the absent ones I love the best
'Neath heaven's smile serenely rest?
Will every branch of the family tree
Still bud and bloom till I am free?

TRUTH.

If they lean upon my breast
I will give thy loved ones rest;
If death a single jewel steal
Heaven its presence it shall reveal.

GUILT.

While prayers ascend from sacred fane
Shall penitent tears be shed in vain?
Will Christ ascend to a prison cell
And deign in a convict heart to dwell?

TRUTH.

None will I spurn who pardon crave—
I came on earth the lost to save;
He loves the most whose debt is large—
That soul is heaven's peculiar charge.

GUILT.

If ever again I shall be free
Will the wreck of my life still haunted be?
Will the much loved friends in the days of yore
Spurn me from their open door?

TRUTH.

Those who bathe in Calvary's stream
Sin regard as a hideous dream;
My children clothed in white by me
A welcome meet where'er they be.

A LETTER FROM HOME.

BY NO. 24138.

I am far from the land where my loved ones are dwelling;
  Between rolls the sea, with its billows and foam;
Yet my heart with fondest emotions is swelling
  As I read the dear letter they've sent me from home.

For I fancy I see the brown cottage again,
  And the garden where sweetly the red roses blow;
I kneel by a grave in the shade of the glen,
  Where slumbers the dear one I lost long ago.

And oft to my heart, when in solitude straying,
  Fond memory recalls the bright days of yore,
And I sigh for the fields, where the children are playing,
  The hills and the valley I may never see more.

Long years have I wandered, alone and a stranger,
  And dark is the pathway o'er which I must roam,
But I know there is ONE who can shield me from danger,
  And his blessing I ask on the dear ones at home.

THE REFORMER.

BY SAM LAW.

All grim and soiled and brown with tan,
   I saw a strong one in his wrath
Smiting the godless shrines of man
   Along his path.

I looked: aside the dust cloud rolled—
   The Master seemed the Builder too;
Upspringing from the ruined Old
   I saw the New.

Through prison walls, like heaven-sent hope,
   Fresh breezes blew and sunbeams strayed.
And with the idle gallows rope
   The young child played.

Where the doomed victim in his cell
   Had counted o'er the weary hours
Glad school girls, answering to the bell,
   Came crowned with flowers.

REFLECTIONS.

How pleasant it is to be at home,
   Surrounded by those we love;
How sweet to list to words of cheer
That softly fall on the listening ear
   Like the notes of a cooing dove.

Iow the soft caress of a loving hand
   Can dry the eyes that weep!
How the mind is eased and the pulses thrill
As we feel the strength of a loving will
   That rocks our grief to sleep.

How soft that hand has ever been
   When sickness laid us low,
How its soft caress could summon rest
And bring relief to the laboring breast,
   And cool the fever's glow.

How soft the light in love-lit eye,
   That welcomes our safe return;
How the tender kiss and warm embrace
Can soothe the pain of late disgrace
   When fate has been too stern.

God bless the home where love abides—
   'Tis the dearest spot on earth!
Be it hovel or palace, or great or small,
It holds man's hope, his joy, his all,
   And heaven gave it birth!

THE PRISONER RELEASED.

BY COL. H. C. PARSONS.

   I could stand and look at the stars all night—
Where tides run in wreaths to the rivers and rills,
Where the sea breezes play with the wind from the hills—
Where by land and by sea man can go where he wills—
   I'm a free man again, and a free man of right.

   I could stand and look at the stars all night,
For months that were years they have prisoned my stars;
My silver-veiled Venus and red-hooded Mars
Were fettered and framed by the merciless bars,
   That shaded their glory or shivered their light.

   I will stand and look at the stars all night;
I will wait in the shadow and lee of the tower
Till morning shall come, with his magical power—
Perhaps in the flame of that wonderful hour
   The prison shall tremble and pass from my sight.

PRISON PAINS.

BY HARRISON.

Oh! to be heart hungry,
   To feel that never again
Shall the heart pulsate with rapture
   To the music of love's strain!

To feel o'er the senses stealing
   A grief for words too deep,
And know the heart's best instincts
   Are locked in fathomless sleep.

To hear the piteous wailings
   That rise from an empty heart,
While every breath is torture
   And every thought a dart.

Oh, list to the wondrous music
   As it floats from the world above:
"There is balm for the broken-hearted:
   The gift of my Son is—love."

Aye, prayer to heaven ascending,
   Tho' winged from a convict cell,
Shall find in heaven a welcome
   No tongue can ever tell.

THE UNDER DOG.

BY BARKER.

I know that the world—the great, big world,
   From the peasant up to the king,
Has a different tale from the tale I tell
   And a different song to sing.

But for me—and I care not a single fig
  If they say I was wrong or am right
I shall always go in for the weaker dog,
  For the under dog in the fight.

I know that the world—the great, big world—
  Will never a moment stop
To see which dog may be in the fault,
  But will shout for the dog on top.

But for me—I never shall pause to ask
  Which dog may be in the right—
For my own heart will beat, while it beats at all,
  For the under dog in the fight.

KINDNESS.

BY ROTH.

A kind word for the prisoner.
  A smile to cheer his heart,
For he bears a grievous burden,
  Tho' he bravely plays his part.

From the world he hides his sorrows,
  Stifles the groan of distress
That struggles oft for utterance
  Beneath his convict dress.

The alert night watch could tell
  Of the burning sighs they hear
While making midnight rounds
  Through corridors so drear.

Then cheer his lot with kindness,
  E'en though he be depraved;
If, wakened from his blindness,
  The worst one may be saved.

THERE IS NO DEATH.

There is no death! The feeble body, slumbering,
   Seems but to waste and fade away;
In future years that God is numbering
   'Twill spring from slumber and decay.

And clothed with beauty everlasting,
   With not a stain of earth to mar,
'Twill voice a music more entrancing
   Than anthem of the morning star.

A thing of beauty is immortal;
   Each line once lost to mortal sight,
Soars upward to heaven's august portal,
   Glad to escape earth's cankering night.

Earth's best and brightest can not perish—
   Death is decreed alone to strife.
The good we love and fondly cherish
   God has endowed with endless life.

Grieve not for those now calmly sleeping,
   Rocked by the slow, revolving earth:
Angelic hosts around them sweeping
   Shall wake them to an endless birth.

In heaven above there is no seeming:
   God feeds immortal souls on bliss;
On earth we linger, sadly dreaming,
   Till death awakes us with a kiss.

Then fear thee not death's friendly slumbers:
   Guardian angels watch thy rest;
Jehovah all thy days shall number
   And do for thee whate'er is best.

DREAMS.

Dreams are but glimpses of the power
   Deep hidden in the human soul
That, like some enchanted flower,
   Withers 'neath reason's stern control.

They come not as invited guests
   To while away the tedious hours—
Are they not lights from heaven sent
   To teach the soul its wondrous powers?

And best they love to lead us back
   O'er scenes to memory doubly dear,
For those we, waking, love the most
   In dreams will seem most near.

While reason sleeps the soul, awake,
   Lives o'er each precious hour,
And woos us with a gentle strain
   Of pathos and of power.

Dreams index to our waking thought
   Plans on which the heart is set,
And he who heeds their warning voice
   Has in life least to regret.

In waking hours we sow the seed,
   In dreams we reap the grain:
Sometimes the harvest all is joy,
   Sometimes, alas! 'tis pain.

What marvel then that sleep is sweet,
   If dreams bring bliss to view—
Perhaps the afterglow of death
   Will prove most dreams are not untrue.

THE GREAT "O. P."

"Forward, march!" the left foot first,
   The heel down mighty hard,
Your head erect and turned to the left,
   As you slyly watch the guard.
Tramp, tramp, three times each day,
   Back and forth to our meals,
While the fellow behind, with his "State brogans,"
   Scrapes the skin all off our heels.

The visitors in amaze at us gaze
   As we march gayly by,
The ladies fair, with many a stare,
   Will slyly say, "O my!"
Some "Hayseed" old, with a chronic cold,
   Will suddenly say, "I swow!
There goes the man—do you see him Ann?—
   What took our brindle cow!"

They say we are "cut-throats and "robbers,"
   And would be worse if we could;
But it's false—we're noble-hearted patriots,
   Here for our country's good,
And the honor came to us, you know;
   We didn't go to it
In other words, we were forced here
   To "do" our little "bit."

Uncle Sam's domain has been ransacked
   For men with blue-blooded veins,
For we don't want any persons here
   With any mortal stains.
We are all old sons of Irish lords—
   Or at least we'd like to be—
But instead we are only "cons," you know,
   Doing time in the great "O. P."

Coming In and Going Out

BY CARR.

Coming in to penal slavery,
  Coming in from liberty;
Going out to joy and freedom,
  Going out the world to see;
Coming in, oh, how unhappy!
  Going out with many a doubt—
Endless stream of wretched mortals
  Coming in and going out.

From the many charms of home life,
  From beneath the humble cot,
To this penal institution
  Where the felon mortal's brought
From some distant homes perhaps torn
  Because grim justice took a fit—
Coming in with sighs and sadness,
  A bondsman for his life or "bit."

Far his loving wife and children,
  While their eyes with tears are wet;
Though his family needs him daily,
  And there are bills that must be met,
To this convict world about us,
  With its heartless woe and din,
Endless stream of restless mortals
  Adding to its load of sin.

Time goes on so very slowly,
  Though we try hard not to grieve
For the dear old family homestead
  And for those we're forced to leave;
Weary are we very often,
  Weary when we try to win
News of those who loved us dearly
  Ere we took this step in sin.

Coming in, alas! to never
  See the outside world again!
Some there are that have my pity:
  Naught for them but toil and pain;
Doomed life's golden hours to fritter
  Far from home and friends most dear—
God's pity on the poor full-termer
  Coming in to die, we fear.

Coming in to serve our sentence,
  Going out, we hope, to cheer;
Coming in to do hard labor,
  Going out to family dear—
Careless stream of wretched mortals
  From all stations 'long life's route—
Hovel, mansion and the hamlet—
  Coming in and going out.

SOUL SCULPTURE.

BY BISHOP DOANE.

Sculptures of life are we as we stand,
  With our souls uncarved before us,
Waiting the hour when, at God's command,
  Our life dream shall pass o'er us.
If we carve it, then, on the yielding stone
  With many a sharp incision,
Its heavenly beauty shall be our own,
  Our lives the angel vision.

WEIGHT AND IMMORTALITY OF WORDS.

Who knows how heavy his words may be,
Or watches, when he has set them free,
Their poising, their flight, their rise and fall
In the world of thought? We are careless all.

We fathom our own, not another's mind,
And are all near-sighted among our kind,
While words of ours and words of theirs
Are meeting and wrestling unawares.

Words are types of our moral trend,
The blooms of our daily lives, that lend
To others the fragrance of what we are—
The outward semblance that goes afar.

The part of ourselves that is not our own,
When set afloat in the vast unknown,
The something we give to the moving wheels
Of the mighty force that grows and feels.

No words are lost as they float away:
On some life ever they rest and weigh,
Unbound in public or depths obscure
Their immortality is secure.

Deep in our hearts we often find
Words lips long closed have left behind:
They live in the chambers of the brain,
The source of endless joy or pain.

Words may be soft as evening air
Or fierce as sultry noonday's glare,
But soft or fierce, be sure they rest
A curse or blessing in some one's breast.

How deep soever their meaning may lie,
Not every soul will pass them by!
No anger, nor passion, nor malice so great
But a match 'twill meet in a world of hate.

No love so deep, no word so kind
But lodges at last in a kindred mind,
No thought so vast, nor high nor low
But a parallel meets in a world of woe.

A heedless word a heart may break,
A thoughtful one a fortune make;
One, hurl a soul in endless night;
Another, lead to heaven's delight.

One word may nerve a murderer's arm,
Another still a raging storm—
One, sow the seeds of endless strife;
Another, sanctify a life.

Our words outline the feeble tongue
From which their outward being sprung,
Or, written on the stainless page,
They live to bless or curse an age.

How careful, then, ought we to be
Before we let such engines free!
Once free, no power can call them back,
Nor human genius trace their track.

We loose them 'mid the wide expanse
'Neath joyous spell or sorrow's trance,
But if their fruitage all could know
We would not deem them half so low.

WHICH LOVED HER BEST?

Two votaries of love's maddening dream
At twilight sat beside a stream,
Each painting scenes of future bliss,
Dependent on their darling's kiss.

Both were young and both were fair,
With noble hearts and manly air,
And both were members of a band
Who bled to free his native land.

Each was bound both heart and soul
Beneath fair Nellie's sweet control,
Yet they were friends both true and tried,
If such ere lived, if such ere died.

Each loved her much, yet neither knew
How well each loved her, nor how true,
For each was dreaming of the hour
That *he* would cull this priceless flower.

At last Ned turned and gayly said,
" Next Wednesday I and Nellie wed—
God knows I am the happiest man
In all this joyous Western land.

"I could not keep this back from you—
That would be unjust—untrue.
I feel whatever shall betide
That *you* will e'er defend my bride."

Harvey turned aside his face,
Lest his friend should see some trace
Of the anguish and despair
The hopeless suffering mirrored there.

Each word had sunk within his heart
Like adder's tooth or poisoned dart;
Joyful love and hope had fled,
And left his withered heart—stone dead.

He raised his haggard face above
Until an angel mother's love
Sent comfort to her suffering child,
That made him calm and meek and mild.

By memories of the tented field
Where patriots died, but dared not yield,
He knew that Ned his arm had lent
To stop steel for his bosom meant.

And oft had watched beside his bed
When others in dismay had fled;
When he spoke, his voice was low
And soft as rippling streamlets flow;

"I wish you peace and joy, Ned;
You best deserve this queen to wed.
I only crave in future life
To serve you and your peerless wife."

The loyal look in Harvey's eyes
Was to Ned a new surprise;
And in a moment all was plain—
His friend's devotion and his pain.

They stood and wrung each others hand
To reinforce their friendship's band—
Their hearts were full, their eyes were wet,
Yet who can such a scene regret?

Their friendship stood the cruel test,
And sank triumphant into rest;
They parted, but to meet again
Where life was torture, memory pain.

One year passed, and war had swept
O'er the spot where these two wept,
While they, with Meig's galland band,
Were held by Santa Anna's hand.

Behind Satillo's gloomy walls,
Whose history stoutest heart appalls,

Here base deeds were hourly wrought
With hell's intensest malice fraught.

Two hundred patriots true and tried
To Santa Anna's shame here died
Simply because they leapt the wall
And strove to go beyond recall!

Ned and his comrades planned their flight
While careless sentries slept at night,
And in safety reached the distant plain
Where hope and life revived again.

Across the arid plain they sped,
Half clothed, half starved and almost dead;
Without a guide to lead them right
They toiled by day and prayed by night.

The blistering soil bold cactus bred
Till every toil-worn foot was bled,
And one by one the hapless band
Fell prostrate on the glittering sand.

Pursuing soldiers found them thus,
And drug and drove them to the "truss,"
There to await the "tortures grand"
That Santa Anna would command.

"Nine of ten shall now be shot;
Choose the guilty dogs by lot:
This law for ages now untold
Has defied both fraud and gold!"

Nine black beans and *one* snow *white*
Were placed within a box at night—
Every captive must draw one,
Blindfolded, ere the work begun.

If *white*, he lived, if black, he died—
Thus were the Texas patriots tried!
By sons of Gantimozin's race—
Man's caricature and heaven's disgrace!

Harvey drew one of faultless white,
Ned drew one as black as night.
"I'm lost—oh, God, my wife!" Ned gasped,
As Harvey sprang his hand to clasp.

"Not so," he cried, "your bean is white
See, mine is *black*, thank God! 'tis right!"
E'er Ned could draw a conscious breath—
Harvey had met a hero's death!

Which loved her best, the man who *died*
Or he who *lived* to cheer his bride?
Please answer me; O heart, awake—
Such liberty I dare not take.

THE STORMS OF LIFE.

BY SAM LAW.

The oak strikes deeper as his boughs
  By furious blasts are driven;
So life's vicissitudes the more
  Have fixed my heart in heaven.
All gracious Lord, whate'er my lot
  In other times may be,
I'll welcome still the heaviest grief
  That brings me near to Thee.

LOVE'S VICTIM.

She was no dainty city belle,
 Half art and half deceit,
And yet no fairer vision
 The human eye could greet.

Naught knew she of city life
 Or fashion's changing art—
Nature created her a belle
 And blessed her with a heart.

Her eyes were large and soulful,
 Her face divinely fair;
Her form was lithe and graceful
 And a golden dream her hair.

Her voice was full of melody:
 Each tone to listening ear
Seemed to awake such music
 As angels delight to hear.

Beautiful, pure and guileless,
 With the faith of a trusting child,
She worshiped the God of nature
 With a spirit undefiled.

She lived with honest parents
 In a home on the mountain side,
Where peace and plenty lingered
 And love was true and tried.

Parental duress was unknown,
 For love's restraints are mild:
A mother's love and father's hope
 Were centered in this child.

The acknowledged belle of the mountain,
 She spurned the coquette's art,
Determining never to promise
 Her hand without her heart.

She could not love her suitors
  With the love a wife should give,
And deemed it sin without such love
  In wedlock's bonds to live.

The idol of many a noble heart,
  None dared their suit to press;
Thus they wound the gentle spirit
  That pitied, but could not bless.

Grateful for each friendly smile
  That o'er her face would beam,
She reigned an empress absolute
  In each fond lover's dream.

A petted child of fashion,
  The heir to boundless wealth,
Came one day among them
  To recruit his waning health.

These hospitable mountain people
  Welcomed the haggard boy,
And strove to make his visit
  One radiant scene of joy.

They bade their darling daughter
  To be the stranger's guide,
And show him all the beauties
  Of her loved mountain side.

Together they scaled the mountains,
  With many a merry shout;
Together they garnered the flowers
  Or angled the nimble trout.

He spake of his home in the city,
  Of the wealth he soon would own;
Promised to make Lenora his wife
  Ere the summer days had flown.

Lenora loved this stranger
  With a soul-absorbing love,

And trembled 'neath his caresses
  As helpless as a dove.

He was a master of the art
  That robs the halls of Truth
To gain what passion courts,
  Tho' it blasts the hopes of youth.

His honied words of flattery,
  Uttered with seductive art,
Were music to the listening ear
  And soon deceived the heart.

Lenora confided in his worth,
  Receiving each promise as truth—
How could she doubt her only love
  In the trustful hours of youth?

Assured of an early marriage,
  She yielded to him one day
That priceless germ of innocence
  And fell—to trust a prey.

She hoped this sacrifice would gain
  Her lover's every thought;
This were a boon, if death could buy.
  She deemed not dearly bought.

Little she dreamed that fatal hour
  That love had sped the dart
That stamped her as an outcast,
  With a withered, broken heart.

Eugene went to his city home,
  Swearing to soon return
And claim as wife the girl he knew
  His parents proud would spurn.

Summer and autumn days passed by
  And the winter's cold set in,
Yet the recreant lover came not
  To the child he taught to sin.

A mother's ever watchful eye
   Discovered her daughter's shame,
Heard her story with breaking heart,
   But uttered no word of blame.

She knew her daughter's downfall
   Was the fruit of love beguiled,
But hated the heartless stranger
   Who ruined her trusting child.

God alone can measure the pain
   That child and mother felt,
As, locked in lingering embrace,
   In agony they knelt

And poured in heaven's listening ear
   Their heart-destroying grief;
And who so bold as to deny
   That Heaven sent relief?

The father learned his daughter's sin
   And drove her from his door.
"Go!" he said, "you guilty wretch,
   You are my child no more."

Stung by these cruel, terrible words,
   She fled in wild affright
In search of the heartless lover,
   Her fearful wrongs to right.

She tracked the guilty miscreant down,
   And he, to save his name,
Hid her till her child was born
   In a house of doubtful fame.

The world looked on the helpless child
   With cold, unpitying eye.
The villian bade his dupe go home,
   "Repent of her sin and die."

She heard, and from her glittering eye
   No tear of anguish sped—

With dagger drawn she reached his side,
   And struck the villian *dead!*

With her babe she sought her father's door
   And pled with a piteous cry
A shelter for her hapless babe
   While the storm was raging high.

"Begone, you wretch!" the father cried,
   "I curse the hour that gave
Birth to a wretch whose sin has laid
   My wife within the grave."

"My mother dead! and I still live?
   Ah! whither shall I fly?
O God! protect my hapless babe,
   And suffer me to die."

The storm increased; she wandered on
   Almost till break of day,
Till weary, wet and almost dead,
   She knelt in the path to pray.

The sky was lit from end to end
   By the lightning's awful glare,
And a falling tree pinned both to earth
   As they knelt in the act of prayer!

They found them thus in the morning light,
   And the father's grief was wild.
He tenderly looked on the touching scene
   And at last forgave his child!

They buried Lenora and her nameless babe
   Close beside her mother's clay,
And each one spake in kindly tones
   Of the hapless ones that day.

The arm that sent the dagger home
   Was nerved by a brain dethroned;
'Tis Lenora's was an awful deed,
   But her terrible death atoned.

Aye, let us hope the much-wronged child
　　Has reached a home above
Where babes can live who have no name
　　And 'tis not sin to love.

A PRISONER'S LAMENTATION.

A poor convict in his cell lay dying;
　　He thought of home and loved ones dear.
He asked his cell-mate, in a whisper,
　　"Do you think the end is drawing near?"

"If I should die before I see them
　　Tell them how I longed to-night
To have my mother's blessed care
　　To leave this world of sin and strife."

Oh! how he longed to see his mother
　　And the cottage on the hill—
"*God bless them all,*" I heard him whisper,
　　As with tears his eyes did fill.

"Will they think of me—a prisoner—
　　I, who was once their pride and joy?
While I sleep in the churchyard yonder
　　Will they think of their wayward boy?

"I know I've caused them lots of trouble
　　In wild and reckless boyish day,
But I hope that God will now forgive me
　　When from this earth I'm called away.

"I know it broke my mother's heart
　　When she heard of me, her wayward son,
Who five long years did serve in prison
　　For a highway robbery he had done.

"Has Sister "Minn," whom I used to play with
　In days of youth, forgotten me?
If she has, I vow I can not blame her,
　For I've caused her pain and shame, not glee.

"There's but one wish I now shall mention—
　That Mother's days may be days of joy,
And when she asks for me in prison
　Speak mildly of her convict boy.

"Here, take this to my dear old mother!
　I know 'tis but a lock of hair,
But it's all I've got to give her now—
　I know she'll treasure it with care."

And when he handed me the keepsake
　His spark of life had nearly fled,
He clenched my hand and uttered "*Mother!*"
　And a poor convict there lay dead.

May all young men now take fair warning
　From one who's had experience long;
Guard strong against temptation's dawning—
　Cast off evil and do no wrong.

In your younger days *court* good, *shun* evil;
　Be careful who you companions choose;
When you make life's start then do not cavil—
　March manfully on to win, not lose.

OUR BOARD OF MANAGERS

Long have we lived in misery and woe;
Long have we suffered from " kindness " cold as snow;
Long has pernicious influence been kept
Hovering 'round our misery, while in dungeons we have slept.

Long have we suffered from want of human care;
Long have we been bearded as the tiger in his lair;
Long have we went hungry for want of proper food,
And felt the sting of th' master's lash, as o'er our task we stood.

As the dark and gloomy cloud, that hovered o'er our past,
Has been wafted off by humane hands—'tis swept away at last.
We now emerge from darkness into a welcome light,
And live in brighter future hopes—a day made out of night.

We hail you, noble, honest men, whose hearts beat five as one,
Thus far in your prison work your duty you have done;
Eternal God will always right the brutal wrongs of man,
And therefore He did send you here to do the best you can.

A Cherrington, for the chairman, is a master stroke, you know,
And a Rose is always welcome, 'cause virtue he will sow;
A McConica, of democrat fame, is a power behind the throne,
While a Hoffman, sent from Cleveland, is a father to the home;
A Muscroft from old " Cincy " is a rattler for the place;
They all do join their hands and thoughts and duty bravely face,
While a McAdow records their acts with a gentlemanly grace.

They issue mandates right and left and order what is just;
They raise poor fallen, helpless man to a place of welcome trust;
They seek to lead him on the way to a nobler, better life,
And restore him to his children and his broken hearted wife.

Their Coffin always sits close by to lend a helping hand,
And faithfully their trust does keep—a leader of their band.
Well they know the awful fruitage of each harsh and brutal plan
Is to rouse the lurking tiger in the breast of erring man.

Now they rule, whose every impulse ripened by enlightened
    thought,
And it leads to many actions that with highest good is fraught.
And they use with great discretion measures that are just and
    kind,
Hoping to reform the erring through the agency of mind.

They have learned the useful lesson taught men from the power
    above,
That the greatest force in nature is the power of inspired love.
They have learned that rank dissension from all evil nature flows,
And they deem that man the greatest who can ease most mortal
    woes.

Let us ever sing enchanting of our now official corps
As they lift us from dark ruin as it has been heretofore.
See! the clouds so lately darkening o'er the prisoner's gloomy
    past,
Mercy's hand is fast dispelling—REASON *takes the reins at last!*

A TRIBUTE TO

ASSISTANT DEPUTY WARDEN L. H. WELLS.

BY G. W. VAN WEIGHS.

Comrade, may the God of heaven ease the maddening pain
That has swept across your bosom since your son was slain;
Think not of him as a mortal mouldering into dust; —
God, too, loved him and, my comrade, He betrays no trust.

You shall see him when the morning breaks above the night of
    death,
And your parting, O, my comrade, will but seem a passing breath.
Well I know the awful pressure grief exerts upon the soul,
But I know it will but whiten what it can't control.

You have met on field of battle many a gallant foe,
And, with patriotism burning, gave them blow for blow,
You have fought till every rebel bent the suppliant knee,
And the land you loved and cherished once again was free.

You despise no gallant fellow who once wore the blue
When it cost both blood and treasure if a man was true.
You forgive the trivial errors of that noble band,
And you meet a loyal comrade with extended hand.

You have friends in every station where your worth is known,
You have showered acts of kindness that but few have known,
Since your advent in this prison you have daily won
Hearts that ever will remember *acts of kindness nobly done.*

Comrade, time is passing swiftly, and Jehovah his reveille
Soon will sound upon the hilltops of a vast eternity.
May we gather with our comrades on that ever beautiful shore
And, like conquering heroes, listen to Heaven's plandits ever
  more.

ONE AND A FEW.

BY 21069.

Of all the pet pleasures so pleasing to man
  In his present degenerate state,
I doubt if there's any can make him so glad
  As the one I'm about to relate.

While here he's confined he's troubled in mind
  With his "fifteen" or "twenty" to do,
And he longs for the day when he boldly can say:
  "I've only got one and a few."

Then keep a strong heart. With courage don't part,
  But manfully fight your way through;
Be it "five" or it "ten" or twice that again,
  'Twill come down to "one and a few."

How often at night when I sit in my cell,
   After working quite hard all the day,
My memory goes back to the time that I fell,
   For the "bit" which I now have to stay.

And sometimes, I own, while sitting alone
   I feel sad and disconsolate, too;
But it makes me feel gay when I think I can say,
   "I've only got one and a few."

Oh, many's a home that's cheerless tonight,
   And many's the mother feels drear;
When she thinks of the one far away from her sight
   It causes her many a tear.

Though others may cleave to her, you are the same;
   Misfortune but makes her more true;
She may now be quite sad, but won't she feel glad
   When you've only got "one and a few?"

Then, don't be discouraged. No matter how long
   In this prison you may have to stay,
You know that to worry and fret is quite wrong,
   Far better drive dull care away.

Old Time is the boy your "bit" to destroy
   As he jogs along, contented and true;
And so, in the end, you'll find he's the friend
   That brought you to "one and a few."

MIDNIGHT MUSINGS.

'Tis midnight! The sentry's muffled tread
   Is heard within these walls;
As silent as the living dead
   He makes his regular calls.

I try to sleep, but all in vain;
   I try to close—I weep,
I hear that muffled tread again—
   The sentries on me peep.

I hear a voice so clear and plain
   It calls to me aloud—
It calls to me again, again;
   That voice comes from a shroud.

Hist! Hist! vile heart, be still! No fear,
   My angel sister's voice I hear!
It speaks to me in accents clear
   And bids me shun a vile career.

She bids me meet her once again
   And live in Heaven's fairest clime.
Nor shall her pleading be in vain—
   Resolved, I'll do no crime.

Oh, could I feel her warm embrace
   As when, in days of old,
I gazed into her angeled face—
   It gave happiness untold.

Oh, let me live my boyhood days
   As in the time gone by!
And let me consecrate her ways
   When for this boy she'd cry.

But, hist! again the muffled tread
   Comes gliding, silent as the dead,
Along the beat within these walls—
   Hark! Hark! again dear sister calls.

A QUERY.

BY MORSE.

When the long weary days are over
   And the front gates open to you,
Are you again to be a wild rover?
   What are you going to do?

Have you plans or dreams for the future?
   Have the days any brightness for you?
Will you be a poor homeless creature?
   What are you going to do?

Should your old-time friends forsake you—
   Those who were strong and true—
And leave you helpless, homeless—
   What are you going to do?

But you have one friend who is faithful,
   Who is always kind and true.
Read His word and study His gospel—
   He'll tell you what to do.

STRAY THOUGHTS.

In the fathomless depths of the mighty deep
What wonders live, what mysteries sleep!
What mind can name the sightless things
That live in the ocean's hidden springs,
Where treasures heaped on treasures lie,
Forever secure from the human eye;
Where creatures sport, that God alone
Can know their joy or hear their moan?

Who knows but the bride of the Dublin Bay
May walk in the ocean's depths today,
Arm in arm with her own dear Roy
In the conscious flush of honeymoon joy?
Who knows but the hearts that sadly yearned
For the gallant ship that never returned,
Have met, in the ocean's unknown bed,
The loved, tho' lost, we all thought dead?

Science has proved the human frame
Is water and salt by another name!
Hydrography yet may teach mankind
The open door of heaven to find.
"Davie Jones' locker" may prove to be

Instinct with life, by death set free!
Knew we the tongue of the deep sea shell
What wondrous news its notes might tell!

The myriad stars in yonder skies
May be the beams of death-freed eyes
That watch us from an unknown shore,
Still faithful to the vows of yore!
The vaulted blue of heaven may be
The looking glass of the mighty sea,
Where deathless souls their vigils keep
O'er fast decaying world, asleep.

Atlantis, the fabled city of old,
Whose gates inspired poets behold,
May now be resting beneath the wave,
Triumphant o'er a watery grave!
Its pearly gates and glittering spires
Arouse the poet's mad desires.
He sees—and sings in tongue unknown—
The mysteries by the Muses shown.

Conducted by a sybil fair,
He penetrates each demon lair
And pictures hell, in golden speech,
Beyond imagination's reach.
To highest heaven his thought has flown
And measured and admired the throne;
Made angels bow beneath his rod
And dared to mould the mind of God!

Who knows but legends the Muses tell
Are truths encased in a mighty dream?
Who knows but the angels of earth and air
Are the beautiful nymphs beside each stream?
Each singing bird and nodding flower
May be imbued with potent power;
And stars an influence, too, may wield
And bless or curse our natal hour!

Who knows but what we call a brute
Is with immortal reason blest?

Who knows man is alone divine
And destined to immortal rest?
Theorize and reason as we may,
How little we can really know;
We only learn to live, then die,
And who may say to what we go?

JUDGE NOT, LEST YE BE JUDGED.

BY SAM LAW.

Art thou so good, so free from sin
That thou should'st judge thy fellow men?
Look well to self before the stone,
Aimed at thy brother's faults, be thrown,
    Behold in thee
    A Pharisee.

If thou art not so low, perchance thou'rt only so from
    circumstance;
Perhaps, if tempted, thou would'st fall. Thy nature's
    sinful, after all.

Thou knowest not, most righteous scribe,
The struggles, trials, patience tried;
The battles fought, the vict'ries gained,
The bleeding heart, the soul tear-stained,
    More human be,
    Have charity.

THE CONVICT'S PRAYER.

BY 21269.

At midnight, in a prison cell,
On bended knee the convict fell,
And poured in heaven's listing ear
A prayer for those he held most dear.

Oh, God; defend my absent wife,
Whose breaking heart and blighted life
Spring not from conscious guilt within.
But from a reckless husband's sin.

Spare her, indulgent heaven, the blow,
That oft has laid an angel low;
Still may her ever angel face
Reflect the presence of Thy grace.

Be it well pleasing in Thy sight
That she may rear my babes aright,
And teach them, in the bloom of youth,
The laws of kindness and of truth.

Help me discharge, on every hand,
The duties right and law demand;
And may I live to dwell once more
Honored among the friends of yore.

PRISON POETRY.

WINE VS. WATER.

There stood two glasses, filled to the brim,
On a rich man's table, rim to rim,
One was ruddy and red as blood,
And one as clear as the crystal flood.

Said the glass of wine to the paler brother:
" Let us tell the tales of the past to each other.
I can tell of banquet, revel and mirth,
And the proudest and grandest souls on earth
Fell under my touch as though struck by blight.
Where I was a king, for I ruled in might.
From the heads of kings I have torn the crown;
From the heights of fame I have hurled men down.
I have blasted many an honored name;
I have taken virtue and given shame.
I have tempted youth with a sip, a taste
That has made his future a barren waste.
Far greater than a king am I,
Or than any army beneath the sky.
I have made the arm of the driver fail,
And sent the train from the iron rail.
I have made good ships go down at sea,
And the shrieks of the lost were sweet to me,
For they said, " Behold ! how great you be ! "
Fame, strength, wealth, genius before me fall,
For my might and power are over all.
Ho! ho! pale brother," laughed the wine,
" Can you boast of deeds so great as mine ? "

The water said proudly, " I cannot boast
Of a king dethroned or a murdered host;
But I can tell of a heart once sad,
By my crystal drops made light and glad—
Of thirsts I've quenched, of brows I've laved;
Of hands I've cooled and souls I've saved;
I've leaped thro' the valley, dashed down the mountain,
Formed beautiful rivers and played in fountain,
Slept in the sunshine and dropped from the sky
And everywhere gladdened the landscape and eye.
I've eased the hot forehead of fever and pain,

I've made the parched meadows grow fertile with grain;
I can tell of the powerful wheel of the mill
That ground out flower and turned at my will;
I can tell of manhood, debased by you,
That I lifted up and crowned anew.
I cheer, I help, I strengthen and aid;
I gladden the heart of man and maid;
I set your close-chained captive free
And all are better for knowing me."

These are the tales they told each other
The glass of wine and its paler brother—
As they sat together, filled to the brim,
On the rich man's table, rim to rim.

THE FALL OF SODOM.

Thou sin-cursed city of the stricken plain,
Whose heinous lust all after time shall shame,
'T was thine to rouse Jehovah's awful ire,
And test the strength of Heaven's revengeful fire.
Thy senseless lust and crime had spread
Till virtue, hope and shame had fled;
Degraded youth and tottering age
Could not appease thy senseless rage;
Thy leacherous sons, that roamed at night,
Were human only to the sight;
Their motto was hell's direst fruit:
"Debase the *man*, exhalt the *brute!*"
One man alone of all thy teeming millions sate,
And pondered on thy sin with deathless hate;
His righteous soul was vexed from day to day,
And strove in vain to turn you from your way.
He dwelt among you as a child of God,
And in the path of honored wedlock trod.
You, dead to nature and to nature's voice,
Spurned woman and made man your choice!
And desecrated, with your impious lust,
The masterpiece God had formed from dust!
Till woman, shorn of all her natural power,
Was cast aside, like some discarded flower,

And stormed insulted heaven with hourly cry.
Till God beheld you with His searching eye,
And sent His angels in avenging haste
Your sin to punish and your land to waste.
The son of Horan met these at the gate,
And begged them at his frugal board to wait;
At first refused, they after turn aside,
And 'neath a righteous roof content abide.
They share his food and list with eager ear
As Lot recounts each nightly scene of fear;
When lust runs riot in the open streets,
And man with man in strange communion meets.
The men of Sodom learn, with kindling eye,
The stranger's presence, and in haste draw nigh.
Men, young and old, with equal ardor burn,
And, with unholy lust, towards these strangers yearn.
They call the patriarch with an angry shout,
And bid him bring the hallowed strangers out,
That they may satisfy their lawless lust
And trample decency in sinful dust.
He, taught from infancy in Mosaic Law,
Regarded heaven's High Ruler still with awe;
And shuddered with indignant fear
As these vile shouts assailed his ear.
He left his house and closed the door behind,
And to the rabble thus he eased his mind:
"Ye men of Sodom! *once* in life do right,
Nor do this wickedness in heaven's sight!
Two virgin daughters 'neath my roof reside,
Till now a father's care and mother's pride;
Take them and do whatever you deem right,
But lay no impious hand upon my guests tonight.
The laws of hospitality, by Moses taught,
Harms not a stranger whom our roof has sought.
They know the law, who now reside within,
And with horror view your awful sin!"
"Ye men of Sodom! who this stranger gave
The right to judge us and our will to brave?
We kindly took a homeless wanderer in,
And dare he brand our greatest pleasure sin?
Shall empty words defy our proud behest,
Or useless offering prevent our guest?
Ten thousand 'No's' will pierce his dastard breast,
And treat him tenfold worse than all the rest!"

Thus spake their leader, and with angry roar
The o'er wrought friends assail the door;
Lot, backward hurled, could hardly stand,
Till snatched within by angel hand,
The maddened crowd no longer wait,
But headlong rush to meet their fate!
The ready angels rise, with godlike mind,
And strike the guilty wretches blind;
In vain they strive to reach and force the door,
Their useless orbs are blasted evermore!
"Go seek thy children, Lot, in eager haste,
And bid them not a precious moment waste.
God will destroy this sin-accursed place,
And wipe from earth its faintest trace!"
Lot, thus commanded, found each one that night,
And faithfully portrayed their awful plight;
But he, to them, seemed as a man that mocked,
And left them sorely grieved and doubly shocked.
The morn arose! The angels cautioned Lot
To wife and daughters take and tarry not;
And as they lingered took them by the hand
And led them from the endangered land.
"Flee to the mountains and no hind'rance brook,
Nor backward turn a long, admiring look.
The wretch who dares this mandate to defy
Shall, 'neath Jehovah's hand, in torture die!"
This stern command was heard by trembling Lot
With deep repugnance, for it pleased him not.
"Nay, nay, my lord: but if before thy face
Thy trembling servant dares to plead for grace,
Command me that I now may turn aside
And in your little city safe reside.
Thus may I keep my soul alive this day
Nor after fall to mountain beasts a prey."
The heavenly strangers, with an august nod,
Agree to lift from Zoar Jehovah's rod.
The rescued quartette Zoarward bend,
While hope and fear alternate tend.
With mien majestic, yes, with hasty tread,
Their trembling flight their aged father led.
Next came the virgins, able scarce to stand,
And followed by their mother, last of all the band.
She yet to Sodom and its idols clave,
And dared Jehovah's awful wrath to brave;

One look she sought, her weary journey to beguile,
And in a moment stood transfixed—*a Salty Pile!*
The more obedient trio onward fly,
Until the opening gates of Zoar greet the eye.
Now, with full hearts, they reach the calm retreat,
And cordial welcome from King Bela meet.

END OF FIRST CANTO.

THE FALL OF SODOM---CANTO SECOND.

From Bera's palace, and from Sodom's shrine,
A thousand scintillating rays of beauty shine;
The gorgeous parapets of beaten burnished gold
Enlightened fancy can with awe behold.
Those marble walls of rainbow-tinted hue,
Please and instruct and yet astound the view.
Each curve of beauty and each line of grace
Relates some annal of the ancient place.
Upon these sculptured walls each Sodomite may trace
The birthplace and the lineage of his entire race.
He here may read, in many a flowing line,
The maiden efforts of the Tuneful Nine,
Who first appeared and strung the quivering lyre,
When new created stars their Maker's praise aspire;
Theirs is the music of the quick revolving spheres,
And theirs the power to bathe a world in tears.
They paint in colors, dipped in liquid truth,
The brow of beauty and the lip of youth.
Thought, tame in prose in their enchanting line,
Is dressed in beauty and is half divine.
They wing love's arrows with consumate art,
And make the melting music of the heart.
Youth they instruct and tottering age sustain,
Virtue exalt and hideous voice restrain.
Inside this palace life is but a dream
Of beauty, flowing in a constant stream.
Here silken curtains hang on wires of gold,
And zephyr-satin, whose capacious fold
Ten thousand giddy turns and windings take
The secret chambers of the place to make.
Each article of comfort man can know
With priceless gems and flashing colors glow;

Each drinking vessel is a solid gem;
Each odorous flower grows on a parent stem;
Birds of bright plumage raise their tuneful note
And scatter scents ambrosial as they float.
The crystal fountains generous wine dispense,
And food delicious satisfies the sense;
The air is balmy as the breath of spring,
And every atom is a beauteous thing.
One thing alone this mighty place appalls:
No woman dwells within these sculptured walls.
Here man with man in lustful caprice plays,
And Heaven's righteous mandate disobeys;
Sinks, through his lust, below the groveling beast,
Who to the female makes his amorous suit.
Within those walls are stores of untold wealth,
Secured by carnage and by midnight stealth;
Beneath each divan and each downy couch
The smouldering fires of retribution crouch.
Each glittering tankard and each costly plate
Reflects the fierceness of each pending fate.
The quenchless tortures of Jehovah's wrath
Is earthward tending in a destined path!
The brilliant sun of light, the mighty sire,
Seems bathed in blood and heaven 's all afire.
From pole to pole the livid lightnings flash
Till all creation trembles 'neath the crash;
And earthward, still, the melting heavens bend,
While blinding floods of hissing flames descend,
And seas of lava, with three mighty bounds,
The now doomed city and the plain surrounds.
Now, inward flowing, rolls the mighty tide,
On whose dread billows death alone can ride;
And upward rising, with tremendous sweep,
Its molten billows awful union keep
With floods descending from the flaming sky,
And Sodom knows her hour has come to die!
Her frightened millions in a circle band,
And view approaching death on every hand.
Around them rolls a sea of fire;
Above them flames the torch of Heaven's ire;
While hissing lava, in descending rain,
Creates new horror and gives birth to pain.
Each gorgeous palace and each mart of trade
Is buried for their wickedness and in ashes laid.

In vain they call their idols, name by name,
Their garments all are wrapt in living flame,
Their quivering bodies tortured to the bone,
Their parched lips in vain assay a moan,
Their eyes still pleading with each bated breath
Not for forgiveness, but for instant death!

The circling oceans, with resounding roar,
Meet and commingle—and the scene is o'er!

A TRIBUTE TO

THE WOLFE SISTERS.

Music, the sweetest all-inspiring gift of God,
  Is ever welcome to the prisoner's ear;
There's nothing makes me feel half so well
  As music of the heart when sung with cheer.

Here in this prison as I sit and pore
  Over the past and present of my life,
My heart sings ever, o'er and o'er,
  The darkest bitterness of a prisoner's strife.

But hark! in yonder chapel shrine
  I hear sweet music as of yore;
I ask, "What music is that sounds so fine?"
  The answer comes, "The Wolfes are at the door!"

I hasten, then, to brush my prison garb,
And toilet try to fix as best I can,
And then unto the chapel wend my way;
When there upon the rostrum stand
      Five of the sweetest singers of our day!

There's Amy Wolfe, who changed her name to Brooks;
She leads her choir without the aid of books,
She sings with voice so sweet and delicate
That to her, First Soprano I dedicate.

Next, Minnie S., at the age of twenty-three,
Sings like a lark and busy as a bee,
Carefully guarding that no mistakes are made,
And handles her bewitching voice with harmony well staid.

Then sang the sweet Zoraydo F., with baritone most clear,
Who, at the age of twenty, delights to bring us cheer,
It seems as if her heart and soul were bent on doing right,
And when she sang she sang so sweet—Oh! it was out of sight.

The next I saw was Lyda M., with scarlet cheeks aglow;
She sings with voice most charming, a clear and sweet alto,
She's next the younger of them all, because she's just eighteen,
She captivates the heart of man—what a fairy little Queen!

Then last, not least, the little one, that is, Miss Kittie C.,
She just so busy when she sings she's like a honey bee.
Her eyes are clear as crystal, her locks are flowing gold,
She sings soprano quite as fine as any I have told.

I sat down in an empty seat close by the outside door,
And listened to such warbling as I never heard before.
Their voices drowned all sorrow and gushed forth many a tear,
Not for horror that I felt—it brought me real good cheer.

They drove away the pain of woe, that none but prisoners smart;
They sang the ever blessed song—true music of the heart.
We doff our striped caps to you, O girls of sweetest song,
And may we bid you be our friends and return again ere long.

Adieu, adieu, our lady friends, do not now say "farewell."
Because we wish you all return with song too sweet to tell.
Come back! come back again and sing some lovely Sabbath day,
For your presence here to sing good cheer we all will ever pray.

And now unto the aged Wolfes please let me say one word:
Your home must be a palace filled with sirenic good;
Proud may you feel and justly, too—of these five daughters fair,
And great the good they've done for us while in this prison lair.

There's but one wish that emanates from a prisoner's wicked
    heart,
That is to say, without delay, "May heaven take their part,
And to them bring eternal joy that 'll pierce them like a dart!"
Each song they sing is welcome here—a masterpiece of art!

And now to part we sadly must (while I'm immersed in prison
    dust),
But hoping, too, 'twill not be long ere you return with sweetest
    song. Adieu! Adieu!

PRISONERS.

God pity the wretched prisoners
   In their lonely cells today;
Whatever the sins that tripped them,
   God pity them still, I say.

Only a strip of sunshine
   Cleft by rusty bars;
Only a patch of azure,
   Only a cluster of stars.

Once they were little children,
   And perhaps their wayward feet
Were led by a gentle mother
   Toward the golden street.

Therefore, if in life's forest
   They since have lost their way,
Whatever the sins that tripped them,
   God pity them still, I say.

TWO LETTERS.

BY GEO. W. H. HARRISON.

I wrote a letter while jealous rage
   In my bosom reigned supreme;
The words were fraught with anger,
   And a loathsome disesteem.

They fell on the pure white paper
   And marred its stainless page,
Yet eased my maddened spirit,
   And appeased my senseless rage.

I gloatingly tho't of the dumb despair
   That letter would surely give,
To one who had broken her faithful vows
   In a way I could never forgive.

I doubted not the perfect truth
   Of all I heard them say;
She, like other girls, was false
   While her lover was away.

I knew she vowed she would be true
   While life itself would last,
Yet thought that she, like others,
   Too soon forgot the past.

I hastily sealed the cruel note,
   And placed it next my heart,
Determined upon the morrow
   To give it an early start.

I threw myself upon the couch
   And sought for sweet repose,
And in my restless slumbers
   A vision then arose:

I saw in that terrible vision
   A woman whose eager face

Beamed with yearning, restless love
   As her trembling fingers traced

A message of love and tenderness
   To her loved one far away,
As her pure lips quietly murmured,
   "God grant we must some day!"

She sealed her letter with dainty hands,
   And laid it by with tender care;
Then humbly kneeled beside her bed,
   And poured her soul in prayer.

She prayed for her impassioned lover
   In a warm, impassioned strain,
That proved her heart both warm and true
   And free from guilt or stain.

She arose from her kneeling posture,
   To answer a call at her door;
She smiled as she saw the letter
   The hand of the servant bore.

One glance she gave—then burst the seal
   With trembling, eager haste,
And rapidly heard the cruel words
   My reckless hand had traced.

Her lovely face turned deathly pale
   As she wildly clutched the air,
She tottered and fell—a senseless heap—
   A prey to dumb despair.

So still she lay I deemed her dead,
   And sprang to raise her in my arms.
I loved her with the old, wild love,
   And bowed to her peerless charms.

"Speak! darling, speak!" I wildly cried,
   "Pray, come back from the voiceless shore.
I cannot, dare not live an hour,
   Unless I hear your voice once more!"

She opened wide her lovely eyes,
   And cast on me one lingering glance
So full of injured innocence
   It smote me like a lance.

I seized the heartless letter,
   Curst cause of all my shame,
And, with one imprecation,
   Consigned it to the flame.

She watched me with a languid smile,
   And pointed to her heart:
"You have destroyed the proof," she said,
   "But can you ease the smart?"

"I have been true to all my vows,
   Heaven judge me if I lie!
But since you deem me to be false,
   Go—leave me here—to die!"

At last I woke and quickly drew
   The accursed sheet from my breast—
Burning it with a ready hand—
   And gently sank to rest.

I wrote another, whose tender words
   Were soft as the ripple of a stream;
And thought what a contrast it would be
   To the letter she read in my dream!

And my darling greatly wonders
   Why my letters with tenderness teem,
Since I have never told her
   Of the letter she read in my dream.

A PRAYER FOR JUSTICE.

Oh, God in heaven up on high,
How long this cruel strife?
Must I but perish in this den
To end this wretched life?
Is there no justice here on earth?
Must truth remain crushed down
And vile and wicked, cruel man
Forever look and frown?
Is there no power to bring to light
The *truth* of my offense?
Must perjury and bribery
Prevail forever hence?
Can enemies, vile, cruel things,
Twist truth all out of shape,
And cause one who's not guilty
To morally wear death's crepe?
Oh, God! is there no remedy
For earthly subjects thus
To be relieved from wretched pain
Without this earthly fuss?
Oh, God! to Thee we call for help.
Wil't thou but listen—hear?
Look down upon me as I be,
My innocence thou 'lt surely see,
These shackles, bolts, and prison bars,
The heavy locks and massive key—
Hear, Oh, God! Oh, hear my prayer
And set this captive free.

BIRTHDAY MUSINGS.

BY G. W. VAN WEIGHS.

Just sixty years ago today
   Mine eyes first saw the light;
Now age, with ever onward tread,
   Presages coming night.

Ah! is it night? Or shall it be
   That morning's light shall break,
And from my soul such music bring
   As earth could never wake?

Where are the friends of earlier years—
   Sleep they to wake no more?
Or do they walk with joyful tread
   Heaven's ever radiant shore?

If death is but oblivion's gate,
   Why younger grows the soul with years?
Whose are the faces that we see
   When melts the hearts in tears?

Oh, whence the strains the soul can hear
   When all is hushed in sleep,
And none, save God and angels, near
   When souls their vigils keep?

Is all religion but a myth?
   Are all our hopes in vain?
Is heaven affectation's child,
   Born of disordered brain?

Tell me not such bolts and bars
   Can keep me from the skies;
I'd sooner deem yon blushing rose
   A satyr in disguise.

A TRIBUTE TO
THE WOLFE SISTERS

BY GEO. W. H. HARRISON.

Come, O come, ye radiant sisters, heaven honored "Tuneful
   Nine."
Smooth my ever rugged numbers and inspire my drooping line.
Aid my muse to tell the story, never breathed to mortal ear,
How this sweet angelic chorus happens to be lingering near.
In yon fair and blissful aiden, far beyond the faintest star,
Once the guardian angels slumbered, leaving heaven's gates ajar!
And five wandering seraphs wandered, in their rapid, noiseless
   flight.
Thro' the gates, whose vaulted arches echoed pæans of delight!
Quick as thought their tireless pinions clave the unresisting air,
Till they reached the *five Wolfe sisters*, maids of form and fea-
   tures fair,
And within these hearts they lingered, tuning every chord to
   song,
Till the pathos of their music stilled the ever restless throng!
Earth and heaven stood astonished and Jehovah's love decreed:
"Let them stay! such strains seraphic mortal beings can but
   heed!"

Have you heard their wondrous music? Have you felt their
   sweet control?
If not, friend, you 've scarcely sounded half the mysteries of
   your soul!
Amy, soul-enrapturing artist, sweetly sounds the soft prelude,
And beneath her skilfull fingers every note, with life imbued,
Stills the throng, whose very silence is an encore loud and deep,
And each thought, save that of music, is forgotten or asleep.
Katherine's rich and full suprano, like the Autumn's mellow
   morn,
Wakes the slumbering soul to action like the practiced hunts-
   man's horn!
Mamie's soft, melodious voice nobly takes the second part,
And the pathos of her music captivates the raptured heart!
Lida's faultless second alto deepens all the noble strain
Till the mind forgets its madness and the heart rejects in pain.

Then Zoraydo's matchless voice sweeps the soul along
Till we know that *perfect music can be breathed in earthly song!*
Hear, O hear the melting music pouring from each heaving
breast;
How it wakes the heart to rapture! How it soothes the soul to
rest!

When they sing, such lovely visions seem to rise and grandly
float
Like the poet's airy mansions, on the wave of each full note!
Silvery daybreaks brighten slow; sunsets blush on mountain
snow!
Moonlight shivers on the open sea; Autumn burns in bush and
tree;
Blowing willows bend and sigh; whispering rivers wander by;
Thro' the pines sweep sea-tones soft; sailing birds shout loud
aloft;
Strange notes beat the lambent air; visions float divinely fair;
Vanished faces come and go; silenced voices murmur low;
Gentlest memories come and cling, *as we listen and they sing.*

Oh, repeat the music's tale, "*Love shall perish not nor fail!*"
We forget the fear of death—breathe, in tho't, immortal breath!
We believe in broadening truth; trust the generous creeds of
youth;
Feel consoling hopes that climb up to some triumphant clime,
And sweet dreams of splendor bring *as we listen and they sing!*

Walls of rock and bars of steel we can neither see nor feel;
We forget our dire disgrace; disregard both time and place;
Bid all angry passion sleep and profoundest silence keep!
Hoard the trembling notes that fall like an angel mother's call;
Rise above our low estate and forget the wrongs of fate!
We forgive our mortal foes, source of all our many woes,
And penance itself loses half its sting, *as we listen and they sing!*

May the God of love and truth give them all the joys of youth;
May the raptures they impart ever thrill each noble heart;
May their ministry of love lead all erring ones above;
May wealth, happiness and joy all their waiting hours employ;
Be their cares both light and few and their pleasures ever new;
And their lives one dream of ease till their "ship comes o'er the
seas!"

Let fate oft their presence bring, *and we'll listen while they sing!*
Gentle sisters, take this tribute poured from imprisoned hearts;
You have eased their maddening torture, *you* have stayed the cruel darts
That remorse and shame have driven deep within each captive soul.
Suffer them your names to graven on fond memory's deathless scroll;
Be assured your seeds of kindness shall not fall on stony ground,
Many of your willing converts have both peace and pardon found!
And, when all your work is ended, you in heaven shall fondly greet
Some whose hearts were first enlightened by your anthems clear and sweet.

TO A DEPARTED IDOL.

BY G. W. VAN WEIGHS.

Thou art not dead, thou art not gone to dust,
   No line of all thy loveliness shall fall
To formless ruin, smote by time and thrust
   Into the solemn gulf that covers all.

Thou canst not perish. Tho' the sod
   Sink with its violets closer to thy breast,
Tho' by the feet of generations trod
   The loadstone crumbles from thy place of rest.

The marvel of thy beauty cannot die;
   The sweetness of thy presence shall not fade;
Earth gave not all the glory of thine eye;
   Death cannot smite what earth ne'er made.

It was not *thine*, that marble forehead pale and cold,
   Nor those dumb lips they laid beneath the snow;
Thy heart would throb beneath that passive fold;
   Thy hands, for me, that stony clasp forego.

But *thou* hast gone. Gone from this dreary land;
  Gone from the storms let loose on every hill;
Lured by the sweet pursuasion of a band
    That leads thee, somewhere, in the distance still.

Where e'er thou art, I know thou wearest yet
    The same bewitching beauty, sanctified
By calmer joy, and touched with soft regret
    For him who seeks but cannot reach thy side.

I keep for thee the living love of old,
    And seek thy place in nature, as a child
Whose hand is parted from its playmate's hold
    Wanders and cries along a lonesome wild.

When, in the watches of my heart, I hear
    The messages of purer life and know
The footsteps of thy spirit lingering near,
    Life's darkness hides the way I fain would go.

Canst thou not bid the empty realms restore
    That form, the symbol of thy heavenly part?
Or in the barren fields of silence pour
    That voice, the perfect music of thy heart?

Oh, once—once bending to my warm and eager lips,
    Take back the tender warmth of life from me,
Or let thy kisses cloud with swift eclipse
    The light of mine, and give me death with thee.

ACROSTIC TO WARDEN AND MRS. E. G. COFFIN.

Elijah of old ancient times was a man of many, many minds!
Long did he live in noble deeds, in dealing comfort to men's needs.
In these, our modern, modest days, all men have greatly changed their ways—
Jehovah's laws do not control the wickedness of every soul.
All those who know as well as I while on this earth will not decry
He who will bad men reform—Hail, Coffin! who for us was born!

•

Godfrey is his second name, and now he reaps most enviable fame;
Our watchword is both day and nights—while o'er him floats the Stars and Stripes—
"**D**o unto us as you would choose, that others do to you and yours!"
Faithful to her life-long trust, a wife, a mother, true and just,
Resolves to help both maid and man and lend an ever helping hand—
Each day and night they toil and pray for boys and girls to mend their way,
Yet they do not toil all in vain for the great good done the human train.

"**C**offin" is a word some shun, for it takes man when on earth he's done
But to the churchyard laid in clay, for ages sanctioned such a way.
For us poor sinners here in "hell" a Coffin sent makes us feel well.

For often he does ease the pains we feel in both our hearts and brains.
In endless joy may they have peace for kindness they have done to us—
Not one of us, though cursed with sin, will e'er forget our friends Coffin.

Canto Second---Last, But Not Least!

Mistress she is of the Coffin shrine, and so it's been for years of time!
In holy wedlock girls and boys have been the idols of their joys!
She bids her Lord Elijah bide a faithful servant by her side,
To aid her with a helping hand to raise poor, wretched, fallen man.
Real sympathy for the prisoner's woe, she seeds of comfort tries to sow
Ere long before it is too late to save poor sinner from his fate;
She "cookies" make, with pearls all set, and puts them in Elijah's hat,
She then does send him on his way, while for the prisoner she does pray.

Mary silently did keep the watch o'er Christ while he did sleep;
All her *protege* she will save if her Lord will help her brave
Roaring storms of vice and ire, kindled by a vengeful fire!
You may guess for all the rest, let *me* say SHE'LL DO HER BEST!

Coffins, to you let us turn! and all crime forever spurn!
Only aid us in this strife to fight manfully for life.

Father Elijah! Mother Mary! for our welfare do not tarry!
Fear you not! for the good you've done has saved many a fallen one!
In our hearts we oft despair as we linger in this lair—
Not for long tho' when we've seen—Father Elijah and Mary, his Queen!

A PRISON VISION.

BY GEO. W. H. HARRISON.

'Tis midnight in these prison walls,
   And even the sentry's muffled tread
Sepulchral sounds, as if he trod
   The silent confines of the dead.

In vain I close my weary eyes,
   I cannot sleep tonight;
I hear an angel's rustling wings
   Fresh from the realms of light.

A sacred presence haunts the air,
   A messenger from Heaven's own land;
And memory awakes again,
   Touched by an angel's wand.

I seem to hear, deep in my soul,
   The music of a heavenly choir,
While each pulsation of my heart
   Awakes in me the old desire

To see once more that lovely form
   Death vanished in my arms;
To hear again her melting voice
   And revel in her charms.

To feel the tender, soft caress
   Of a loved tho' vanished hand,
And hear from her departed lips
   The mysteries of that land

That lies beyond Time's rugged shore,
   To all unknown, save those
Whom angels capture for the skies
   At life's uncertain close.

I muse again, with loving thought,
   Of a sinless wife long dead,
And live again our buried past,
   By an angel presence led.

I view again the pleasing scene
   Of a school house on the hill,
Where happy scholars daily met,
   Whose law was the teacher's will.

I see again the old armchair
   Where the Master daily sat
With watchful eye and helpful hand,
   Yet sleepless as a cat.

I hear again the sleepless hum
   Of voices low and sweet,
Of students pouring o'er the books
   With wisdom's germs replete.

Amid that happy, guileless throng,
   There was one peerless face
That held in the Master's tender heart
   An undisputed place.

It was a face, O God! how fair!
   No words can ever paint;

More fit for heaven than for earth,
  It bore the contour of a saint.

The brow was high and broad and white,
  With a radiance all its own;
The cheeks, like lilies dipped in blood,
  Were oft as a rose full blown.

Eyebrows dark and delicately arched,
  Were penciled in Nature's play;
The ruby ripeness of her lips
  Seemed never to melt away.

Her lustrous eyes, whose depths were brown,
  Yet seemed a darker hue,
Were windows of a spotless soul
  That scorned to be untrue.

Abundant tresses of dark brown hair
  That almost swept the ground,
Enveloped as chaste and lovely form
  As e'er on earth was found.

A voice so soft, so sweet, so low
  That every accent woke
Sweet notes of blissful melody,
  As if an angel spoke.

None could look upon that face
  And deem that aught of earth
Could chill the rapture of a soul
  Where sin could know no birth.

Her mind had wondrous power and scope:
  It grasped the sea, the earth, the sky,
And rightly understood and loved
  The God who ruled on high.

Contentment, truth and virtue
   Was part of Nature's dower;
Self-sacrifice to her was joy,
   And prayer was conscious power.

While yet a child her spirit soared
   Above the things of earth,
And mused with soulful tenderness
   On the heaven that gave it birth.

The teacher's stern, imperious heart
   Yearningly worshipped this child,
And 'neath her hallowed influence
   Grew tender, warm and mild.

The haughty heart, that never sought
   The plaudits of the world,
Poured its richest tribute
   At the feet of this faultless girl.

The face, that never even blanched
   'mid war's terrific strife,
Grew pale as death the hour he asked
   This child to be his wife.

No word she spake, but simply laid
   Her head upon his breast.
He folded her in warm embrace
   And knew that he was blest.

Each lived a life of conscious joy;
   Earth seemed a garden fair;
The lover sought earth's fairest flowers
   To braid in her shining hair.

Deeply they drank at the font of love;
   Draughts few natures can hold;

The hours were seasons of perfect bliss:
  Each moment more precious than gold.

Days and months flew swiftly by
  On the wings of happiness sped,
And two sweet babes were garnered
  As the fruit of their marriage bed!

They neither thought nor dreamed of aught
  Save their babes and coming bliss;
They greeted the morn with soft caress
  And welcomed night with a kiss.

Till, thundering on the wings of Time,
  Fate dealt the cruel blow
That dashed a home in pieces
  And laid a child-wife low.

The husband pressed her to his breast
  And fondly kissed his bride;
But with the parting of that kiss
  The sinless child-wife died.

The kindred angels joyful flew
  From the realms of endless day,
And gently wafted her soul above,
  But left to us her clay.

"She is dead! Kiss her and come away.
  Your cries and prayers are all in vain,
Your May-Bell is cold, senseless clay;
  In heaven above you'll meet again.

They smoothed her tresses of dark brown hair
  Back from her marble forehead fair;
Over her eyes, that oped too much,
  They closed the lids with a tender touch.

They closed with tender touch, that day,
The thin, pale lips where beauty lay;
About her brow and her sweet pale face
They tied her veil and bridal lace;

Placed on her feet the white silk shoes
That May-Bell for her marriage chose;
Over her bosom crossed her hands;
"Come away," they said, "God understands."

With bowed heads they left the room,
Still shuddering at its silent gloom;
And naught, save silence, lingered there
Around the corpse of May-Bell Clare.

But I loved her far too well to dread
The silent, stately, beautiful dead.
I cautiously opened the chamber door
And was alone with my dead once more.

I kissed her lips, I kissed her cheek,
But 't was in vain, she could not speak.
I called her names, she loved, awhile,
But she was dead and could not smile.

And not one passionate whisper of love
Could call her back from her home above.
"Cold lips," I murmured, "breast without breath,
Is there no voice, no language in death?"

Dull to ear and still to the sense,
Yet to the soul of love intense!
See, I listen with soul, not ear;
What is the secret of dying, my dear?

Was it the infinite wonder of all
That you could let life's flower fall?

Or was it a greater marvel to feel
The perfect calm o'er agony steal?

Was the miracle greatest to find how deep
Beyond all dreams sank down that sleep?
Did life roll back its record, my dear,
Showing all past deeds dark and clear?

Oh, did love, sweet mistress of bliss,
Affrighted, vanish to shun death's kiss?
For radiant ones in the world above
Forget those whom on earth they love?

Oh, perfect death! Oh, dead most dear,
I hold the breath of my soul to hear!
I listen as deep as fathomless hell,
As high as heaven, nor will you tell!

There must be pleasure in dying, my sweet,
To make you so placid from head to feet!
I'd tell you, darling, if I were dead
And *your* hot tears on *my* cheeks shed.

I'd speak, though the angel of death had laid
His sword on my lips, their accents to shade.
Not in vain should you, with streaming eyes,
Beg to know Death's chief surprise.

Oh, foolish world! Oh, precious dead!
Tho' you tell me, who will believe 't was said?
Who will believe I heard you say
In your own dear, kind familiar way:

"I can speak now—you listen with soul alone;
To the eyes of your soul *all* shall be shown.
In this land of infinite bliss
The utmost wonder, dear one, is this:

"I see and love and kiss you again;
I smile at your triumph over pain;
I know your heart is honest and true;
I'm a guardian angel to you!

"What a strange, delicious amusement is death!
To live without being, to breathe without breath!
I should laugh did you not cry;
Listen, dear one, love never can die!

"I am now your heaven-decked bride;
My body and not my love has died!
Dear one, *it* lies there, I know,
Pale and silent, cold as snow.

"And you say, 'May-Bell is dead.'
Weeping o'er my silent head!
I can see your falling tears,
Hear your sighs and know your fears!

"Yet I smile and whisper this:
I am not the clay you kiss;
Cease your tears and let *it* lie,
It was mine, but 't is not *I!*

"Dear one, what the women love
For its silent home, the grave,
Is a garment I have quit,
As a tent no longer fit.

"'T is a cage from which, at last,
My enraptured soul has passed.
Love the *inmate*, not the *room*,
Love the *wearer*, not the *plume!*

"*Love* my *spirit*, not the *bars*,
That kept your May-Bell from the stars;

Be wise, dear one, and quickly dry
From every tear your laden eye.

"What you place upon the bier
Is not worth a lover's tear;
'T is an empty shell at last,
Out of which the soul has passed.

"The shell is broken, *it* lies *there*,
But the *pearl*, the *soul*, is *here!*
'T is an earthen jar, whose lid
God sealed when it faintly hid

"The soul He made to live on high;
The mind that did not, cannot die.
Let the dross be earth's once more,
Since the gold is in His store.

"God is glorious! God is good!
Now His word is understood!
Life's ceaseless wonder is at an end,
Yet you weep, my erring friend!

"See, the lover *you* call dead
To immortal bliss is wed!
Loves and homes you lost, 't is true,
To such light as shines for you.

"Yet deep in your inmost soul
You shall feel my sweet control.
I 'll be with you every hour,
Commissioned by Almighty Power.

"To guard each moment of your life
As best befits your angel wife!
At night I 'll linger 'round your bed,
With an angel's noiseless tread;

"And while you, slumbering, dream of me,
I'll be present, love, with thee.
Where e'er you go, where e'er you stray,
I'll be near thee night and day.

"Guarding you with zealous care,
Pointing out life's every snare,
Chasing every tear away.
Aiding every joy to stay.

"Chide you when you go astray;
Bless you when you kneel to pray;
Lead you, with an unseen hand,
To view the wonders of a land

"Where Peace and Love and Perfect Joy
Tongue cannot name, nor peace destroy!
Shall ever bless the happy band,
As radiant 'round the throne they stand!

"Once there, we'll never part again.
But *time*, and *love* while God shall reign.
I cannot, *dare not*, say farewell;
Where I am *now* you, too, shall dwell.

"I am gone before your face,
A moment's time, a little space.
When you come where I have stepped
You'll greatly wonder why you wept!

"You'll know by Love Eternal taught
That Heaven is *all*, that earth is naught.
I beg you not to dread sweet death;
'T is but the first and faintest breath

Of the life that God hath given
To fit immortal souls for heaven!

Be *certain*, darling, *all* seems love,
Viewed from the higher courts above!

"The cares and troubles that arise
Will prove sweet blessings in disguise;
They 'll waft you to a home above,
Where I 'll await your coming, Love!"

I heard these words and fell on the breast
Of the peerless bride that heaven had dressed.
I yearned for those blissful regions above
With heart overflowed with passionate love.

My peerless flower, tho' nipped in youth,
Perennial shall bloom in the Garden of Truth!
I see in the distance a roseleaf hand
Beckoning me on to that glorious land.

Tho' parted on earth we 'll meet in the sky,
Where bliss cannot perish, and love cannot die,
Oh, bliss supernal! Oh, rapture complete,
When earth-sundered ones in glory shall meet.

For years and years I 've watched in vain
To see that buried face again;
In vain I've tried, with mortal eyes,
To pierce the mysteries of the skies!

Oh, sweetheart of the days of yore,
Shall we meet on earth no more?
Shall I languish all alone
Without one sympathetic tone—

One glance of love, one word of cheer
From eyes and lips I hold so dear?
Oh, hearken to my piteous cries,
Beloved one, and forsake the skies!

Oh, listen! Earth-born mortals, see!
My angel bride has come to me!
The self-same face—divinely fair—
And heaven-set jewels decked her hair.

Her laughing eye and glowing cheek
Eternal youth and bliss bespeak;
My head is pillowed on her breast,
My brow by her dear hands caressed!

The dulcet tones of her dear voice
Bids my aching heart rejoice;
She folds me 'neath her dazzling wings,
While all the heart within me sings!

Oh, list those melting tones of love,
More soft than note of cooing dove!
Oh, hear the words her dear lips speak:
"Death, dear one, is the boon to seek!

"False are the glittering gems of earth,
Eternity's gold is the gold of worth;
One moment in heaven is worth a life
Spent on earth 'mid care and strife!

"Death is but the dawn of day,
Destroying naught save worthless clay!
The soul lives on in rapturous bliss
More perfect than a virgin kiss!

"Oh, dear one, still your haunting fears;
The love, tho' lost, of earlier years
Awaits your coming to the skies,
And o'er you watch with jealous eyes.

"Lest earth detain you till too late
To enter heaven's wide open gate.

Oh, tarry not on earth too long,
But with me join immortal's song!"

She spake, and through the vaulted sky,
Beyond the reach of mortal eye,
She wings her rapid noiseless flight
And I am left alone tonight.

Nay, not alone; for in my soul
I feel a new-born sweet control
That lures me to a higher life,
Which will please an angel wife!

Farewell, prison blight and bars,
Mine is a home beyond the stars.
Welcome, Death, at any hour,
Since sin has lost her maddening power!

ACROSTIC TRIBUTE TO

CAPT. J. S. ACHESON.

BY GEO. W. H. HARRISON.

Just consider, for one moment, all the good this man has done.
In full many a field of battle he the victory hath won;
Swept he with victorious Sherman from Atlanta to the sea,
Ever acting as a soldier, from all fear and malice free;
Proving true in every station, like a soldier tried and true,
He has earned and won the friendship of the boys who wore the
    blue!

Since his advent in this prison he has, with impartial mind,
Made it plain that every duty can be done and still be kind.
In his bosom rests no malice towards a single human soul;
'T is his study, night and morning, all his passions to control.
He is willing every prisoner should become his honest *friend*,

And the prisoner's reformation he regards as *law's best trend;*
Crime, he deems is but the fruitage of conditions time can change.
He would lift his fallen brother and no rule of right derange!
Ever ready with the welcome of a smile and word of cheer.
Some may only be respected, but such men are ever dear.
O'er the path of life may Heaven scatter roses at his feet;
None will doubt that every christian shall *his* face in heaven
    meet.

MY MOTHER.

CARR.

One bright Sunday morn, as I sat in my cell,
   My thoughts to the outside did roam;
The sweet songs of birds, as their notes rose and fell,
   Turned my mind to my childhood's dear home.

Long years they have passed since I saw that dear spot,
   But its sweet memories time can ne'er smother;
I can never forget that dear little cot
   And the sweet loving smile of my mother.

In sickness or pain 't was dear mother that brought
   Her sweet self and her charms to allay it;
She learned me a prayer and she lovingly taught
   Me to kneel at her knees and to say it.

God's word she would read, and impress on my mind
   The love that's conveyed by that story
Of the Savior, who died that millions might find
   Eternal rest in His realms of glory.

For years she's been dead, and her low, grassy mound
   Reminds me that 'neath it lies sleeping
The dear friend of my youth, whose magic, I found,
   Could bring smiles to my face e'en when weeping.

'T is thus the dear birds, as they joyfully sing
   And chirp happy calls to each other,
Remind me that perhaps they were sent for to bring
   A message to me from my mother.

But, alas! as I think, upon my mind there quickly falls
   The thoughts of my sad degredation;

The strong iron bars, and the grey, sombre walls,
  Recall me to my sad situation.

But no more will I sin: I'll live upright for sure;
  My passions and temptations I'll smother;
And when God calls me home to that bright shining shore
  We'll be happy together, dear mother.

A MEMORIAL ODE.

BY G. W. VAN WEIGHS.

Again the sacred day has come
  When tears and flowers shall fall
On the graves of our sleeping heroes
  Who died at Liberty's call.

And the tears we shed above them,
  As our hearts with tenderness bled,
Is the crown of their matchless glory
  And earth's divinest mead.

Their deeds on the field of battle
  Were such as a god might do,
And the listening angels applauded
  The work of the boys in blue.

The flag they died defending
  Still floats above their grave,
And is loved by millions of freemen,
  But never looked on by a slave.

The country they loved and bled for,
  Still true to her sacred trust,

Will cover their names with glory
 And revere their hallowed dust.

The comrades who still survive them,
 Like gold in the furnace tried,
Speak, with tear-dimmed lashes,
 Of the gallant boys that died.

These flowers will fade and perish,
 Tho' hallowed by each grave;
But they will live forever
 In the hearts of the true and the brave.

Then let this custom continue
 Till tears and flowers shall cease,
And we shall greet the gallant boys
 On the shores of endless peace.

LINES TO MY CELL.

Oh, silent and mysterious cell,
Could I command thy walls to tell
The secrets they have kept so long,
'T would be, indeed, a cheerless song.

A tale of crime, and tears, and pain,
The fruit, perhaps, of frenzied brain,
As none to crime yet ever sank
That had not first become a crank.

" The law of God and man defy,
A wretch you'll live, a felon die!"
These words seem to haunt my brain,
Perhaps it is the sad refrain

Of a song well known to thee;
Yet where its author now can be,
Save thee, perhaps no one can tell,
Thou grim, mysterious, silent cell.

Thy rocky floor has felt the tread
Of many a hapless one now dead;
Thy walls have echoed many a sigh,
Wrung from guilt's expiring eye.

While musing 'mid thy walls tonight
I seem to hear, with some affright,
The wail of many a blighted life,
The prayer of a despairing wife;

A mother, weeping for her child;
A father, grief has driven wild.
And then I pray thee silence keep;
'T were best to let thy secrets sleep.

A TRIBUTE TO

DR. G. A. THARP.

BY G. W. VAN WEIGHS.

Arise, my Muse, and tune your harp
To ring the praises of a Tharp;
His cultured mind and noble soul
Truth and virtue both control.

Tell the world his perfect skill
Can conquer every human ill
That lends to science or to art,
From shattered limb to dormant heart.

Each pill and potion that he makes
Relieves your pain and health awakes;
And should he use the surgeon's knife,
He never will sacrifice a life.

His skilfull fingers place a band
As gently as a woman's hand;
And not one patient needs to feel
That he the truth will not reveal.

The poor regard him as their friend,
And on his bounty oft depend;
Well knowing that his generous heart
Dares to act a christian part!

Long may this noble doctor live,
Ease to suffering men to give;
And meet the summons to depart
With the skill he wooes his art.

AN APPRECIATED FRIEND.

She is a pretty little lass,
   Half human, half divine;
And for an angel she would pass
   In Heaven's lovely clime.

Her hair is locks of flowing gold,
   Her ways are cute and wise;
And her form is lithe and graceful,
   With pretty bright blue eyes.

Her manners are just perfect,
   Her nature kind and true;
She is a real philanthropist
   When charity is due.

She strives to cheer those sad at heart,
   And well she does succeed;
And stays the ever painful dart
   That often fate does speed.

How different from so many folk
   Who frown upon the one
Who, by some simple words he spoke,
   Caused " crime " to have been done.

Although the cruel knife of fate
   Has made an awful wound,
In her kind words, that come but late,
   Sweet balm for sorrow 's found.

Oh, that this wicked, wicked world
   Could boast more such friendly souls!
Less lives would be so sadly hurled
   Into a pit of earthly ghouls,
Where nothing 's saved, but all is lost;

And where man's cast, at any cost,
Into a dismal, prison dell—
A gloomy, dreary, earthly hell!

Come, of such friends arise and sing,
With thanks returned to heaven's king!

* * * *

SALOME'S REVENGE.

Arise, my Muse, spread out thy wings,
 Prepare to soar away!
Tune up thy harp for endless joy,
 And turn night into day.

Go dream of Paradise sublime
 In the old Empire State!
And when you're done return to me
 Your story to relate.

In time gone by—in days of yore—
 There lived, in forests wild,
Two families of ancient stock,
 And each one had a child.

The children of both parentage
 Were born in this country;
They amassed immensely fortunes
 In this America.

The Waddington's were pure Scotch blood,
 And raised one daughter fair;
They gave her name of Sadie,
 She'd blue eyes and golden hair.

Her cheeks were rich with crimson glow.
  Her lips were thin and cute,
And many an anxious lover
  She sternly did refute.

Her dainty hands and flowing hair,
  And graceful curves of form
Would make one's heart quite palpitate
  She carried all by storm.

Trueman Waddington was a man
  Who loved his daughter—heir,
And as he rolled in endless wealth
  He watched his child's welfare.

Their nearest neighbor was St. Lawrence.
  Who lived a little way
Off on the rugged mountain side,
  Where children like to play.

Two children he had buried
  When they were yet quite young.
And now he was a happy man
  'Cause he reared an only son.

This son he named him Trueman.
  Because he liked the name,
And tho't 't would be in honor
  Of his neighbor of the same.

"As an act of kindness and of love."
  Old Waddington did say,
" Because you named him after me
  I pledge my Sade, today."

The two old friends called in their wives
  And asked them to consent

To seal the bargain for each child
   On which they were both bent.

The mothers thought it rather soon
   To tie so firm a knot,
And begged them not to seal their doom
   By such a foolish plot.

But Trueman Waddington was not
   A man to easy quit,
And he argued long and labored strong
   In a half way frenzied fit.

He said: "I know we are both rich
   In lands and kine and gold,
And why not join these vast fortunes
   Before they are all sold?

"You 've named your only son from me;
   True-man it is, *True-Man* he'll be,
And now must I sit by in shame
   And cannot seal my daughter's fame?"

Then spake the elder man St. Lawrence:
   "Dear sir, my neighbor and my friend,
You have my heart and soul and mind,
   And these vast fortunes I will bind

"Together with true chords of love,
   God help our children find
A part their mothers will not take
   In this, to seal their children's fate.

"Now let me, please, suggest a way
   To reach this matter of today;
And we will friendly make the deal
   So lawyers cannot break the seal."

Then Waddington sprang to his feet,
  And warmly did his neighbors greet:
Then shook him warmly by the hand,
  And said, "Come, let us seal the band."

And then with fixed and mellow eye
  He gazed on high as he stood by
His rugged friend and neighbor, too,
  Then St. Lawrence bade him what to do.

"My dear old friend, sit down, sit down;
  'T is easy for us now to drown
All obstacles that 's in our way
  To carry out our plan today."

Then he proceeded to relate
  How easy men in Empire State
Could call in witness to their deed
  And satisfy all fortune's creed.

"Now, look-a-here, my friend St. Lawrence,
  You cannot be too quick
To tell me how we 'll do all this
  And make this bargain stick."

And then the sage St. Lawrence did say:
  "Look here, my friend, here is our way!
I 'll make my will of my estate
  (And that, you know, is very great.)

"Unto your fair and lovely child,
  If she refrains from being wild,
And when she weds she weds my son,
  My noble, brave and kind Trueman.

"Then you, my friend, reciprocate:
  You make your will of this same date,

And seal as I do mine;
  Make True, my son, your legatee,

"And to him give, in simple fee,
  Your lands, your goods, your kine, your cash,
All in one grand and mighty crash,
  If he your daughter weds."

The witnesses were duly called;
  The wills were then prepared;
The testators did sign their names,
  The children they well fared.

The documents were laid away
  In vaults of solid rock;
There safely for the children kept,
  Their heritage of stock.

Years, years rolled on and Trueman grew
  To be a handsome man,
He said: "I 'm bound to be "M. D."
  And do the best I can."

Sadie, on the other hand,
  Grew to be a queen;
And when to college she did go
  Trueman there was seen.

They played at home, when they were young,
  Upon the mountain side,
And never once did they mistrust
  They 'd be both groom and bride.

When Trueman closed his college course
  He off to Gotham went,
To become an adept in his class
  While on his mission bent.

Sadie, on the other hand,
  When she had closed her term,
Returned unto her mountain home,
  For which she hourly yearned.

Two years had changed this happy home
  To one most sadly grieved;
The mother of this lovely girl
  Had sadly been deceived.

She, down upon her death bed lay,
  When in came Sadie one bright day
And gazed upon the shrunken form
  Which now had battled life's hard storm.

Poor Sadie, with a broken heart,
  She did the best to take her part;
But long the sickness did not last,
  Because her mother now soon passed

From time into eternity.
  Where the human soul is ever free.
Trueman now, in city fashion,
  Had let die out his old-time passion

For rocks and rills and mountain side,
  Where dwelt the queen who 'd be his bride.
So much for selfish, erring man;
  He 'll do the best where e'er he can.

Time, time rolled on, when Sadie's sire,
  With renewed youth and boyhood ire,
Took to himself another wife,
  And tried anew to live his life.

The new-made mistress of the home
  (Who had no place she called her own

Was mother of a daughter fair,
  With dimpled cheeks and flowing hair.

The madame's name was Maria;
  Her daughter's was Sarah.
She soon was boss of all the house,
  And Sadie driven like a mouse

Into the cold and cheerless world.
  Sadie, with a broken heart,
Prayed her father take her part;
  But he, with proud and dire disdain,
  Forever did refrain.

Then Sadie, on her mother's grave,
  Prayed loud and long for God to save
Her soul from earthly wreck.
  Then, with a palpitating heart,

With one fond look she did depart
  To battle hard with broken heart;
While daughter and a second wife
  Should all but ruin her young life.

But father did as fathers do,
  When their list of wives have numbered *two*;
He lent his daughter a deaf ear,
  For his second wife he then did fear.

His life was short; he soon became
  A victim to a raging pain,
Which soon relieved him from this life
  And bore him off from life's hard strife.

They laid him low beside his wife,
  The pride and joy of Sadie's life;

But Sadie knew not of the fate
  Her father had so sadly met.

The new-made widow, without tear,
  Prepared to move, within a year,
To far and distant foreign land,
  Where neither had a single friend.

The goods were sold, the stock and kine;
  The lands were leased for a long time;
The two, with pockets filled with gold,
  Sailed for Paris with joys untold.

Young Sarah, who was quite a belle,
  When in old Paris she did swell
Her wardrobe with both silk and lace,
  And numerous paints to ply her face.

She was the very counterpart—
  Although 't is strange to say—
Of pretty *Sadie* Waddington
  In all her dainty ways.

She spread herself around, about,
  In all society's halls,
And never failed, when chance availed,
  To attend the stylish balls.

She was a favorite with them all,
  In fact, the Queenly Belle,
And many a suitor's prayer she heard
  While on bended knee he fell.

One evening while on promenade
  Within society's halls,
She met a handsome, tall young man
  She 'd seen at some of the balls.

PRISON POETRY.

When introduced, both their eyes met,
   She blushing timidly;
He heard the name, "Miss Waddington,"
   Then asked most courteously:

"From what part of America's soil
   Do you and your friends hail?
Or have you lived in Paris long?
   On what liner did you sail?"

She said: "I'm Sadie Waddington,
   From the city that bears my name;
It borders on the old St. Lawrence,
   A river of world-wide fame."

Then spake the handsome gentleman:
   "I, too, am from that place;
And if you are Sadie Waddington,
   I ought to know your face."

Her cheeks grew flushed and flushed again,
   As on her he searchingly gazed;
She looked up in his solemn face
   And saw he was greatly amazed.

It was Trueman St. Lawrence she saw,
   As she gazed on his beautiful form;
She was more than bewitching in her ways
   To capture him all by storm.

The Doctor went to his hotel
   To ponder the matter o'er;
"That's not the Sadie Waddington
   I've seen in days of yore."

His brain was puzzled, his face was flushed,
   He was in a frenzied mood;

He could not fathom the mystery
  To do the best he could.

If that's the girl in days of youth
  I played with on the mountain side.
Before I leave this old city
  I'll make her my darling bride.

So saying, he sank upon his couch,
  And slept in dreams so rich and gay
That loud his servant called and called,
  Because 't was late—far in the day.

That day he had a trip to make
  Unto a neighboring town,
And visited a hospital
  Kept by a Doctor Brown.

In passing from one of the wards,
  While in the open door,
He chanced to turn, and looking back
  Saw, kneeling on the floor,

With outstretched arms and pleading eyes,
  The girl for years he had not seen:
She 'd grown into full womanhood,
  She was a perfect fairy Queen.

"What! what!" he cried, "am I deceived?
  If I 'm my father's son
That girl I see back yonder
  Is *Sadie Waddington!*"

He hastened back to where she knelt,
  And bade her to arise,
And clasped her to his manly breast,
  While tears rose in his eyes.

Then 'tween her sobs and moans and groans
   She slowly did relate
How she was driven from her home
   Back in the Empire State.

She told of awful suffering,
   Of wandering far and near;
Of the death of father and mother,
   To her *all* that was dear.

She told him how she had returned
   Unto her mountain dome,
And as she was told that all had been sold,
   She was left without a home.

The Doctor stood transfixed with awe;
   Listened to her relate
The story of the sale of all,
   Back in the Empire State.

The Doctor said: "My dear Sadie,
   It matters not a bit to me
Whether you have lands, or goods, or gold,
   I have vast fortunes yet untold.

"What's mine is yours; 't is always so,
   My father told me long ago,
Before I left the Empire State
   And came over here to study late.

"I offer you my heart and hand,
   And pledge to seal it with the band
Of holy wedlock, faithfully,
   Now set your heart forever free

"From labor and the toils of life,—
   Come, say you 'll be my darling wife!

I feel a pang about my heart
   That pierces like a flashing dart."

"Oh, True, St. Lawrence! Oh, can it be
   That you do really care for me?
I, who have lived by a false name
   To hide a step-mother's wicked shame?

"For five long years my name has been
   As you directly would have seen,
Not Sadie W., as you have known,
   But the Sadie changed to plain Salome.

"The Waddington I changed, also,
   For the common name of Van Harlow;
Then among strangers I did seek
   For work to do, although 't was meek.

"I came across the ocean wide,
   As servant to a new-made bride;
She was taken sick and died out here
   Before she 'd been a bride a year.

"Since then I 've cared for poor and sick,
   And cannot leave them now, so quick.
I patients have who *must* have care
   Before *I* leave for better fare.

"Now True, my dear, I 'll be your own;
   I 'll make you an ever happy home;
I feel Pa's oft' spoke words are true,
   Trueman 's your name, *True Man* are you."

He pressed her closely to his breast;
   To dry her tears he did his best;
Then gently kissed her burning cheeks
   And bade her wait but a few weeks.

The happiest man in all the land
  Was True. St. Lawrence, with trembling hand,
Who then returned to his rooms rich,
  A restless night to roll and pitch

Upon a bed of faultless down,
  But pains of heart it could not drown.
He lay and mused throughout the night,
  'Cause his future now looked bright.

Sarah Waddington and her mother
  Prepared a party for another.
A gent they wished to entertain,
  'Cause Sarah wished to bear his name.

" It is to be a swell affair,
  So she could safely set her snare
To catch the unsuspecting True,.
  Because he loves and loves but you."

So spake the mother to her child,
  Who seemed delighted—almost wild—
To think that she could play her part
  Without remorse or pain at heart.

The time rolled on, and days were spent
  In fixing up for the event;
The rich were called from every side
  To see Sarah—the would-be bride.

She sent a most bewitching note
  For Dr. ' Lawrence to cast the vote,
Who 'd be the Belle of honor, bright,
  To bear the graces of the night.

The Doctor smiled, as he sat down
  To answer it, without a frown;

And faithfully he did outline,
  In characters most cute and fine:

"My choice is one, and only one;
  And now I've written and 't is done!
As sure as I'm my father's son,
  'T is one— fair *Sadie* Waddington!

"And now, before it is too late,
  There's one request I have to make:
That I be granted then, or sooner,
  To be escort to the maid of honor."

"Your request is at once granted,
  And hope we'll become enchanted;
And with your presence 'll be elated,
  Because, it seems, we are related.

Fair Sarah, then, did make it known
  Real quietly about her home
That she and 'Lawrence, raised side by side,
  Would soon become both groom and bride.

Silks and diamonds bought with gold,
  Gotten from the kine she'd sold
'Way back in the Empire State,
  Where poor Sadie met her fate.

Just one week before the eve'
  When he Sarah would deceive,
Trueman went to see his love,
  Who was pretty as a dove.

"Sadie," said he, "sweet is revenge!
  Let us now your labor change.
The ones who drove you to your fate,
  Away back in the Empire State,

"Are here in Paris this long time,
  And live in luxury sublime.
The gold they got from off your kine,
  It goes for suppers and for wine.

" In holy wedlock let us wed,
  I 'll lead you to a bridal bed;
And then in luxury and state
  We 'll 'tend the ball ere 't is too late.

" I 'll humble them in dust and shame!
  Ah, Sadie, you were not to blame!
We 'll make them wish they 'd never sold
  Your goods and kine for glittering gold!

" Come, darling, now we 'll off today,
  The bridal knot to firmly tie.
Then I your graceful swanlike neck
  With pearls and rubys will bedeck.

" I 'll trim your lovely graceful form
  With richest satin to be worn;
I 'll place upon your tapered hand
  A solitaire, set in gold band.

" Your dainty feet encased in kid
  Of dainty styles, they 're only made
For those who 're called the name of Queens,
  And bought by those who have vast means.

" Then to the ball we 'll proudly go,
  And who we 'll meet I do not know.
I 'll there present to every one
  My bride, *true* Sadie Waddington.

" The shock, so sudden, will be great;
  They 'll quail beneath their hearts own hate

Of being there exposed to all;
  Oh, won't it be an awful fall?

"Come, Sadie dear, revenge *is* sweet!
  Now is our chance to get your mete
Which they have held from you so long,
  And did you such a cruel wrong."

Then Sadie spoke: "Trueman, my dear,
  There's naught I know for me to fear.
Revenge *is* sweet, although 't is queer,
  Revenge I get in Paris here."

They carried out their little plot,
  And never skipped a single jot.
The eve. was fine, the folk were gay,
  And not a thing stood in their way.

It was quite late when they arrived
  At the mansion of the would-be bride.
As soon as Doctor stepped in sight,
  Escorting Sadie—his delight—

Sarah saw the graceful form
  And, with one scream, she left the room,
And fell fainting to the floor.
  They gently laid her on the couch

Before the open door.
  Her mother came in haste to see
What all the trouble there could be,
  And did not see the Doctor's bride

Until she was close by her side.
  And when she saw it was too late,
She gasped: "Oh, Sarah's met her fate,"
  Then fell into a deathly state.

The mother swooned and swooned away
    The entire night and most the day;
And then the Doctor came to say,
    "Her life is run, she cannot stay!"

Sadie, with trained and skillful hand,
    Nursed Sarah back to conscious-land;
Did faithfully the watchword keep
    While often o 'er them she did weep.

And, just before the mother died,
    She Sadie called to her bedside
And begged her to full pardon give
    For cruel wrong she did receive.

Sadie, always so good and true,
    Said she always thought she knew
That the grand day would surely come
    When that great wrong would be undone.

She granted full, complete pardon
    For all the wrongs the dame had done,
And then she spoke kind words of cheer
    Into the madam's dying ear.

With firm-set eyes and drooping chin
    The madame grasped and tried to cling
Unto the hand she once did scorn,
    And drove from home at break of morn.

She then was wrapt in eternal death,
    And from her soul came not a breath.
In casket pure as driven snow
    Unto the churchyard she did go,

And there was laid beneath the clay
    To await Jehovah's Judgment Day.

PRISON POETRY.

All lands and goods and gold and kine
  She left behind for endless time!

Poor Sarah! doomed to awful fate,
  Her mind was left in ruined state;
In raving madness and in strife
  She tried to take our Sadie's life.

The best physicians in the land
  Were summoned forth on every hand
To try and bring her from the strife
  Back to the land of happy life.

Off to an asylum she must go,
  'Cause 't was not safe to leave her so;
And with good care she might regain
  And be relieved from mental pain.

Salome, our faithful lass and bride,
  Resolved to stay by Sarah's side
And help her regain her lost mind,
  And comfort for her she would find.

Nine weeks were spent in mad-house fare,
  Salome bestowing tender care
Upon the one who once did face
  Salome in all her dire disgrace.

When Doctor St. Lawrence saw his wife
  Was bent on battling for the life
Of one who was once her mad foe,
  He said: "All right, it shall be so."

Salome, she clung unto her charge,
  As if she were her dearest friend;
She incurred expenses somewhat large
  To treat her patient to the end.

The Doctor soon began to learn
  His bride and wife would never spurn
The one who once her home did take,
  And drove her off for mere pride's sake.

He asked Salome what she would do
  In case that Sarah did pull through,
And once again her mind regain
  Before they crossed the raging main.

Salome did quickly make reply,
  While glistening tears stood in her eye:
"I'll take her to old Empire State,
  Right to the door where I met fate!

"I'll make her happy, if I can,
  And now I'll form my little plan:
We must, dear True., just do our best,
  And fix her up in a cosy nest.

We will give her a little home
  On the beautiful mountain side;
We will find her a handsome lover
  Who'll be proud to call her his bride.

"We will give them all attention
  That the best of friends could do;
We will *return good for evil*,
  'Cause my mother taught me so.

"Let us show that true religion
  Is the life we ought to live,
And the ways that Christ rejoiced in
  Are the ways to which we cleave.

"Oh, my husband, dearest Trueman,
  I believe in Sarah reigns

The true principle of goodness—
  Let us fan that spark to flames.

"Can I now secure her safely,
  Teach her shun her evil ways
And discard that haughty spirit
  That she learned in younger days,

"I will be the happiest mortal
  Ever lived on mother earth,
And will reach that heavenly portal
  Only reached by second birth."

After coaxing, begging, teasing,
  Sarah consented for to go
Back across the ocean, raging,
  Where her childhood seeds did sow.

When they reached the harbor safely,
  Bag and baggage on the truck,
They cast lots to see what steamer
  They would choose for their good luck.

Doctor got the choice of vessels,
  And he quickly did decide
That the City of St. Paris
  Should take their *protege* and his bride.

Safely in the vessel's cabin,
  Housed in cosy stateroom there,
All were ready for the voyage,
  And did look for cheerful fare.

Out upon the briny billows,
  Just three days and nights, 't was said,
When the night was dark and dreary,
  Trueman rose from sleepless bed.

There was something weighed upon him,
. Something whispered to beware;
He dressed and went upon the deck
   To breathe the crisp sea air.

He paced and paced the vessel's deck
   With long and manly stride;
He went from starboard o'er to port
   And back to starboard side.

He 'd been upon the deck some time,
   And peered into the gloom
As if them something overawed
   And threatened them with doom.

At last, to port, he spied a fleck,
   A dancing on the waves,
And there he plainly saw a deck
   Bedecked with pirate knaves.

The vessel, with a dark-hued hull,
   Bore straightway on its course,
When, "*Hard to port! To port! to port!*"
   Rang out a voice real coarse.

The strange boat glided swiftly on,
   Like a ghost on phantom wings,
While the crisp sea breeze went dancing past
   And through her rigging sings.

The strange boat slipped along, across
   The briny billows white,
And their steamer ploughed and labored hard
   Along its renewed flight.

It was a close and dangerous call,
   Because the night was dark;

Had they collided there, on the ocean bare,
    They 'd went down with their bark.

The voyage, then, to Gotham
    Was stormy and quite rough,
And all agreed, when landed,
    That they had quite enough.

They then all took the railroad train
    North, through the Empire State,
And soon were on the mountain side
    Where Sadie met her fate.

The first place Sadie wished to see
    Was graves of father and mother,
And tripping lightly from the yard,
    She passed out with another.

That bitter morn, with memories fresh,
    When from her home she 'd fled,
She was scorned by one *now* too glad
    To lead her on ahead.

When she approached her mother's grave
    The tears rolled thick and fast,
And by her side poor Sarah stood,
    With memories of the past

A fitting through her guilty mind:
    And then she spoke at last:
"Oh, Sadie, Sadie, what a blot
    Upon my mother's past;

It stings within my guilty heart,
    And would to God I now could part
With half the pain I feel—
    The balm of Christ could scarcely heal."

PRISON POETRY.

She stooped, and silently did press
   Her fresh and rosy lips
Upon the little mound of grass
   "Beneath—dear mother sleeps."

Then Sarah, with most tender words,
   Pressed Sadie to her breast
And with a fervent, heartfelt plea,
   Prayed both them to be blest.

When they returned unto their home,
   Their friendship sealed with silent love,
They could not bear to be alone;
   They felt a power from up above.

Old friends and neighbors, with delight,
   Called on the Doctor and his bride,
And there convened, on the first night,
   A host of friends who're on their side.

There's one among them old and gray,
   Who'd lived right there for all his life:
'T is the elder man and sage, St. Lawrence,
   And he smiles upon the Doctor's wife.

Heir to the Waddington estate,
   Sadie reigns the queen of all;
Her friendship for Sarah was great,
   And sister her did often call.

The Doctor chose to spend his life
   Upon the handsome mountain side
With Sadie, his true loving wife,
   And Father St. Lawrence until he died.

Time rolled around and months flew by;
   Sadie and Sarah, hand in hand,

Sealed by the firmest friendship tie,
  Two of the truest in the land.

There chanced to stroll from distant clime
  A bright young man of Sadie's kin;
Came to visit in Summer time,
  And Sarah was introduced to him.

Sadie tried her best to make a match,
  And championed well her cause;
Sarah viewed it as a catch
  That one very seldom draws.

Though 't was but a short acquaintance,
  Still the wedding time was fixed;
The intended groom had patience,
  'Cause he felt he was not rich.

Sadie, sweet as dewy honey,
  Wishing that her friends should wed,
Proffered home and lands and money
  If the word would just be said.

" I am heir to all this fortune,
  Known as Waddington's estate;
Come, now, Sarah; come, now, Hawthorne,
  Join your hearts ere 't is too late.

" I will give to you a large farm
  Yonder on the mountain side;
I will give you kine and money,
  If you 'll be my cousin's bride."

Sarah spake, with dewy eyelids,
  To the one she loved so dear;
" Sadie, I am anything but worthy
  Of this princely gift, to cheer

My poor broken, wicked heart,
  After I have been so bad;
You should never take *my* part,
  Since *I* took that which *you* had."

Yet Sadie, true to her own passion,
  Promised deed in fee for all,
If Sarah would wed her own cousin,
  Ere the Summer ran to Fall.

So the wedding day was fixed
  When the two should be made one,
And their home, as she predicted,
  Would be deeded as their own.

When at last the nuptial greeting
  Was received on every hand,
The sage, St. Lawrence, came to their meeting,
  The last one left of their quartet band.

The wedding knot was duly tied,
  And the folk were feeling gay;
They were now made happy groom and bride,
  Starting out in life's pathway.

When the ceremony was over,
  And the gifts they were bestowing—
Bridal gifts as sweet as clover—
  Sadie, with her rich hair flowing.

Called the old 'Squire of the city
  That to witness of her signing
The transfer of title fair,
  To the land that lay up there;

When, to her surprise and chagrin,
  Father St. Lawrence, with gentle voice,

Told her that she could not bargain,
  For she had not even choice.

"Now, my daughter, not one farthing
  Of this vast and rich estate
Has been left unto True.'s darling,
  Now, I tell you, 't is not too late.

"All this land you tho't was yours
  By inheritance of your blood,
Was bequeathed by your dear father
  To one you never thought he would.

Now, I 've brought the Judge of Probate
  As an honored guest of *mine*,
That he might reveal the truth,
  That it might be writ in rhyme.

Then, to soothe the disappointment,
  The old judge with silvery hair
Drew from 'neath his outer garment,
  Two old papers kept with care.

One was read by him to Sadie,
  Where her father had endowed
All his lands, and kine and money
  On the one who made her proud.

When this document was ended,
  And was handed to Trueman,
The old sage, St. Lawrence, pretended
  That he enjoyed youth again.

"Read, Judge! read your other paper!
  Tell my daughter here the truth;
Tell her what their anxious fathers
  Did for them while in their youth."

When the document was ended,
   With tears showering down her face,
Sadie, kisses, sweetly blended,
   While she held him in embrace.

Long their fortunes had been blended
   By the signatures alone
Of their fathers in their child days,
   As they played around their home.

" True, my dear; O will you come here?
   Sign this deed! Come quick, O do;
Carry out my simple wishes;
   Sarah is my friend, so true."

" Yes, my darling, this with pleasure
   I will do, to please you all;
It is my most pleasant leisure
   To do bidding at your call."

So, the deed of gift was given,
   And in happiness they 'd start;
From that home they 'd ne'er be driven,
   Life anew to never part.

There in happiness and comfort
   Did they live upon the place
Where the evil of proud passion
   Smothered one in dire disgrace.

Happy was Salome and Trueman
   When they saw their *protege* safe
In the hands of Cousin Hawthorne,
   On the Waddington old place.

Safe within the coils of homelife,
   Safe within the cottage walls,

Safely with a trusting husband,
Safe within their friendly calls.

Thus the vengeance of our Hero
  Was full spent to meet her theme;
Yet so different from a Nero,
  Because she knew she could redeem.

Salome's revenge was to her sweet,
  'Cause she 'd conquered, not cut down;
Now she feared no one to meet,
  Nor would any wear a frown.

Though some years had been so bitter,
  And had fraught such cruel pain;
Now the coldest of the winter
  Seemed like flowery beds of green.

Now, away up on the mountains,
  In the well known Empire State,
Sadie Waddington is living
  In sweet REVENGE, where she met fate.

A TRIBUTE TO

CAPT. GEORGE W. HESS.

BY G. W. VAN WEIGHS.

Almost a decade thou hast battled with a patriot's band,
Whose first duty is devotion to their native land;
And no comrade but is willing, with a ready mind,
To declare thee brave and loyal to all mankind.

In thy country's hour of peril, on the battle field,
Thou wert ever more than willing all her rights to shield,
And, with true and loyal purpose, battled for the right,
Till secession's traitorous banner sunk in endless night!

Duty's path to thee is glory, glory easy won;
For a task so oft repeated is quite easy done;
Yet no one can ever chide, for thy generous heart
Ne'er will crush the poor and helpless with oppression's dart.

Every prisoner knows and likes thee, for thy friendly ways
Must attract their close attention and excite their praise;
And the few who know thee better, as a man of heart,
Would desire no nobler mission than to take thy part.

May you live in peace and plenty, happy with your own,
Till Jehovah's love shall gather 'round His august throne
All who, like you, honest comrade, follows heaven's plan
And respects the rules of virtue and the rights of man.

MY LAWYER.

When grappled in the law's embrace,
Who first betrayed an anxious face
And fain would shield me from disgrace
    My Lawyer.

Who told me I should not confess,
That he would all my wrongs redress
And set me free from all distress?
    My Lawyer.

When, sick in jail, I senseless lay,
Who took my watch and case away,
Lest prowling thieves on me should prey
    My Lawyer.

Who to my wealth tenacious clung,
And for me wagged his oily tongue,
And at my foes hot embers flung?
    My Lawyer.

Who told me he was dreadful smart
And knew the law-books all by heart,
And always took his client's part?
    My Lawyer.

Who, in the court, with peerless pride,
My rights affirmed, my guilt denied,
And swore the State's attorney lied?
    My Lawyer.

And when twelve men, in one compound,
For me a guilty verdict found,
Who came to stanch the bleeding wound?
    My Lawyer.

PRISON POETRY.

Who said my time within the wall
Would be exceeding brief and small,
The minimum, or none at all?
    My Lawyer.

And when the judge my doom proclaimed,
And three long years of exile named,
Who looked indignant and ashamed?
    My Lawyer.

When, at the sheriff's stern command,
I for the train was told to stand,
Who longest shook and squeezed my hand?
    My Lawyer.

Who, when he had me safe confined,
No more concerned his crafty mind,
Nor was, for me, to grief inclined?
    My Lawyer.

Who closed the mortgage on my lot,
And drove my family from my cot,
And left them homeless on the spot?
    My Lawyer.

Who, when of prison clothes I'm stripped,
And from these walls am homeward shipped,
Will get himself immensely whipped?
    My Lawyer.

[Written by Mr. George Gilbert, who died on the 9th of June, A. D. 1890.]

A SAD WARNING.

BY GEO. W. H. HARRISON.

In prison cell, at early twilight,
  Smoking Foesters "Best Cigar,"
Sat a convict, little dreaming
  Aught his perfect bliss could mar.

Round the cell-block, slowly ambling,
  Came a "Screw," on mischief bent,
And his wide, expanded nostrils
  Quickly inhaled the welcome scent.

Wave on wave, thro' latticed iron,
  Smoky clouds rose thick and high,
And the happy convict murmured:
  "Go, ye cloudlets, greet the sky!"

But the cloudlets, incense laden,
  Lingered near the oaken floor,
Till the "Screw," with cat-like motion,
  Stood before the smoker's door.

In the spittoon, charred and sputtering,
  Lay the smoker's joy and pride;
And the "Screw," exultant, murmured:
  "Stackhouse will *this case* decide."

Morning dawned. The "cellar agent"
  Bore the trembling wretch away
To a cellar, cold and gloomy,
  Where the tools of torture lay.

Blows and shrieks alternate sounded,
  And a voice from near the floor
Murmured: "Stackhouse! MERCY! MERCY!!
  P-l-e-a-s-e, sir; *I will smoke no more!*"

From the cellar, shorn and shaven,
  Skulked the cowering "con." away;
And he smokes—but, Oh! how watchful
  Is that victim, who can say?

All ye inmates, take the warning,
  Gushing from a brother's heart:
He who smokes within these portals
  For the dire offense *may* smart!

ACROSTIC TO

J. C. LANGENBERGER,

CAPTAIN OF THE O. P. NIGHT WATCH.

BY G. W. VAN WEIGHS.

Just to all men, to all men kind and true;

Conspicuous as a giant yet comely to the view;

Loved by all who know him, trusted everywhere;
Always more than willing to ease his fellow's care;
Never harsh or cruel, never false or base;
Going in and coming out among those in disgrace,
Earning from each prisoner's heart the meed of honest praise;
None condemn his actions, none despise his ways;
By his children reverenced, by his wife adored;
Every friend is welcome at his ample board;
Rich in all that makes a *man*, poor alone in hate;
God of Mercy bless the man who nightly guards our fate;
Ever may he fill the post that wisdom has assigned,
Ruling all, as now he does, by strength of heart and mind.

SHE LOVES ME YET.

BY GEO. W. H. HARRISON.

Amid the cares and griefs of life,
   One precious thought I'll ne'er forget,
I have a fond and faithful wife,
   For darling Lulu loves me yet.

The bitterest pang that earth can give
   Can never make my soul regret
The fact that I on earth can live,
   While Lulu says she loves me yet.

The sweetest joy my heart could know
   Would prove a diamond yet unset,
Whose radiant light could never glow,
   Like this sweet thought, "She loves me yet."

Should grief deluge my troubled soul
   Till every hour some care beset,
I could defy its stern control
   While murmuring, "Lulu loves me yet."

Should every friend I have on earth
   Each vow of loyalty forget,
I could survive the cruel blow,
   Since darling Lulu loves me yet.

Should earth with one accord combine,
   Sweet Lulu's influence to beset,
It would not change my constant mind,
   If I but felt "She loves me yet."

I care no sweeter boon in life,
   Nor will my heart its choice regret;
I only long to meet that wife
   Who truly says she loves me yet.

ACROSTIC TRIBUTE TO

HARRY SMITH.

BY G. W. VAN WEIGHS.

He is like the god, Appollo, when in days of old
All the hearts of Greece could conquer, yet despised their gold.
Rich in manhood, health and youth, he is ever free
Ready to assist his brother whatsoever his need may be.
You can trust him freely, fully, with your love or gold,

Since his love of truth and honor never can grow cold.
May he ever do his duty and to all be kind,
It is but the noble hearted who can rule the mind,
Trusting, still, his love of country and his love for man,
He may rest assured Heaven will endorse his plan.

THE PHANTOM BOAT.

BY GEO. W. H. HARRISON.

Two lovers once sat dreaming
Of scenes o'ergrown by years;
Sweet Daisy's eyes were eloquent
With girlhood's pleading tears:
Her little hand was lying
Confidingly in mine,
While her silvery voice pleaded:
"Dear one, awake the Nine!"

"Yes, darling, I will rhyme for you;
What legend shall I drew !
Shall I now fold you in my arms
And, drifting down life's stream,
'Mid singing birds and nodding flowers,
Pour forth my soul in love—
In accents soft and tender—
As the cooing of a dove?

Or shalf I tell you, dearest one,
Why yonder's rippling stream
First gained the name "Tululah"
In an age that's now a dream?
Well, now, pillow your head upon my breast,
The legend is weird and wild;
I fear me much its harrowing scenes
Will shock, thee, gentle child.

Will you listen, while we're watching
For the far-famed Phantom Boat?
Perhaps the tale will lead us
To catch the first faint note
Of Tululah's wondrous music
As she floats down this stream,
For, I assure you, darling,
This legend is no dream.

Where now we sit, in days gone by,
The stealthy panther crept,
And bears and wolves in horrid hordes
Their tireless vigils kept;
Turkey, deer and beaver
Were scattered far and wide,
And here the lordly savage stalked
In all his pristine pride;

The Creeks then ruled this forest,
From Suwanee to the sea:—
A haughty, bold and cruel race,
Cunning, treacherous, wild and free!
To hunt and fish, and boast and fight
Were the duties of a brave,
While woman—alas! sweet woman
Was but a cowering slave!

No grant had she to breathe her wrongs
Before the "Council Fire,"
Nor dared she utter a single word
To gain her heart's desire,
Until her savage master
First gave her leave to speak;
Nor dared she then to brave his will
Lest he his vengeance wreak!

Yet ever and anon there rose
A woman, whose proud soul
Ignored those self-created gods
And spurned their base control.
Such was the brave Tululah,
Whose spirit haunts this stream;
In a phantom barge it glides along,
Like a wraith in a troubled dream.

'T is said she haunts this river,
Alone on a misty night,
And that each one who sees her
Is 'palled with strange affright!

And why she haunts this river
Is the burden of my tale,
And none who have a tender heart
But will her fate bewail.

Tululah was Ocala's child,
To whom the Creeks ascribe
The name of the boldest leader
That ever led their tribe!
A savage of herculean build,
With fierce and restless eye,
His haughty lip deigned not to smile,
And scorned to breathe a sigh!

Tululah was his pride and joy,
The only thing he loved on earth,
Since she became an orphan
At the fatal hour of birth!
The superstitious savage
Deemed her mother's spirit nigh,
And thought, who harmed an orphan,
By a spirit hand should die!

She was born, too, "In a Castle,"
Gifted with a "second sight;"
Friends of earth, and sea, and air,
At *her* command would fight.
Her raven locks and soulful eyes,
Her faultless form and peerless face,
And voice of wondrous melody
Awed and charmed her race.

She reigned an undisputed Queen,
All her mandate must obey;
And even the fierce Ocala
Was obedient to her sway.
Yet even she was powerless
To stay the raging flood
Of tireless, deathless savage hate
That sought the white man's blood.

Ocala's hatred of the whites
Was known both far and near;
Brave hunters spake his name with awe,
And women in trembling fear!
At last he grew so treacherous
No white man dared come nigh,
Till a trio of gallant hunters
Determined *he should die!*

They knew 't was a dangerous mission
On which their steps was bent,
Yet the prayers of honest settlers
Their true hearts courage lent.
As they neared the sleeping village,
Where Ocala awaited his doom,
They flitted like weird spectres
In the silent midnight gloom!

There, spread before their vision,
Five hundred wigwams lay;
A savage guerdon of defense
For him they sought to slay.
To the silent village center
Our gallant hunters crept,
To the door of the largest wigwam,
Where proud Ocala slept.

Stepping across the prostrate form
Of the sentinel at the door,
They breathed a prayer for absent ones,
Whom they might see no more.
Three knives flashed in midnight air,
Then fell with a sickening thud,
Ocala, Napoleon of his tribe,
Lay withering in his blood!

But hark! what means that fierce warhoop,
Resounding loud and clear?
'T is the bugle blast that calls each brave
When the paleface foe is near!

Gathering fast in the midnight gloom,
They form "The Circle of Death"
Around the dauntless hunters,
Who stand with bated breath

Awaiting the savage onslaught,
Determined to sell their lives
To the service of their country
And the freedom of men's wives;
While pitying Heaven aids them
By the darkness of the night,
Since not a star will lend its aid
To guide their foes aright!

Now facing North, and East, and West,
They meet the savage foes,
Recruiting Charon's army
By every lusty blow;
But still they come in hideous swarms,
Like hounds let loose from hell,
Till, overborne by numbers,
Our bleeding heroes fell!

All honor to the gallant three,
Twelve braves in silence lay,
With gaping wounds and stony eyes,
To greet returning day!
While yet a score were nursing
Wounds which these heroes gave,
That signed their right to enter
Into an unwept grave!

Ocala ne'er again would scourge
Their country, far and near,
Nor wring from helpless innocence
An unavailing tear!
His death alone destroyed the boast
And stilled the raging flood
Of senseless pride and passion
That bathed his hands in blood!

But, alas, for human prowess,
These deeds but roused the ire
Of savage wretches, who now tried
To vent their spleen *with fire!*
Three stakes were now erected
And fagots heaped around,
While painted fiends in human shape
Exultant, sat aground.

They led the helpless captives forth,
With many a shout and hoot,
And drug them to their awful doom,
Less feeling than a brute!
And first they bound Hugh Cannon,
Whose descendants, love, you know,
I pointed out to you, last Fall,
When we were at the show.

They bound him to the cruel stake
Before his comrades' eyes,
Then scornfully they bade them mark
" How a paleface coward dies! "
Thank God his captors were deceived,
He smiled amid the flame!
And, with his fast expiring breath,
These words bequeathed to fame:

" To suffer in a noble cause
Is sweet beyond compare!
These greedy flames that lick my blood
But light a vision fair,
Where heroism and heroes sweep
The still resounding lyre,
Heaven's harmonies have quenched
The tortures of this fire!

" Tumultuous raptures 'round me roll
Heaven's pearly gates ajar!
My spirit soars on fleshless wing
Beyond the faintest star!

Oh, blissful death; oh, vision fair,
What sweet celestial glories shine,
The loved and lost of earlier years
Are *now* forever mine!"

The savage horde in silence stood
And listened as he sang,
While even their untaught eyes could see
He suffered not a pang!
No yell triumphant smote his ear,
Awe silenced every tongue,
And many a heart beat faster
As he his requiem sung.

Then lionhearted Conway,
Beneath whose eagle eye
Even savage foes once trembled
Was offered up to die!
Defiant still 'mid writhing flames,
He heaped on them his scorn,
And, with true prophetic voice
He doomed their race unborn.

Rejoice! rejoice! ye howling fiends,
Distort your hideous face,
Soon the white man's wrath shall sweep
From earth your blood-stained race,
While shining fields and cities fair
Attest the white man's power,
You accursed Creeks shall be
Tradition's useless dower!"

Now comes your own ancestor,
The gallant, brave McCray,
Who planned this glorious campaign
And led the awful fight.
He was a perfect Hercules,
Cast in Appollo's mould,
With a heart of witching tenderness,
Yet proud and dauntless soul.

Oft had he visited this tribe,
On peaceful mission bent,
And to many a savage
His kind assistance lent.
Yet little dreamed he, at this hour,
One heart amid that throng
Still beat responsive to his own,
Attuned to love's mad song!

Yet, as they bound him to the stake
And raised the flaming brand,
The Chief that held it fell a corpse,
Killed by a woman's hand!
And Indian maiden loosed his bands
And raised her voice on high:
" Who harms my paleface lover
By Tululah's hand shall die!"

Behold, the savage concourse stand,
Transfixed by silent awe,
And gaze upon Ocala's child,
Held sacred by their law!
They feared Ocala's spirit
Might *then* be hovering nigh;
Nor dared to harm his darling child,
Lest he who harmed her die!

The Queen, with head and form erect,
Bore McCray undismayed,
And in her *father's* wigwam
Her wounded lover laid!
Then bending gently o'er him,
Each wound she rightly dress,
And with sweet plaintive melodies
Lured the weary one to rest.

At dawning light McCray awoke,
His Queen still lingering there;
His eyes bespoke his gratitude,
His lips were moved in prayer

For the lithe and graceful maiden
Whose love he knew to be
Pure as early morning's blush,
Yet deathless as—Eternity!

Although once failed, his savage foes
Still thirsted for his blood;
The hate within their bosoms
Was as tireless as a flood.
Not daring open violence,
They sought Oneida's craft,
And 'neath the guise of friendship
Gave the lovers a sleeping draught.

When the mighty god of slumber
Had locked them fast in sleep,
The wily savage entered,
His fearful oath to keep.
They took McCray to the river
In sight of these roaring falls,
Whose sheer descent—two hundred feet—
The stoutest heart appalls!

They bound him fast in a frail canoe,
Set adrift 'mid the current's flow,
Believing his life would be dashed out
On the jagged rocks below.
Then, gladly turning homeward,
A ready lie they make
To appease her burning anger
When Tululah shall awake!

Slowly the doomed man drifted,
Yet faster, at each breath,
The quickening current bore him
To the open gates of death!
Yet still he slept; aye, slept and dreamed
Of the proud Creek's peerless flower
Who, for deathless love of him,
Had braved her nation's power.

Spurned her murdered sire's corpse
And to his murderer clung!
Aye, on the spot that drank his blood,
Love's soothing ditties sung!
Dreamed of the eyes that flashed with fire
When his foeman dared draw nigh,
Yet softened into tenderness
At her lover's faintest sigh.

Dreams of the hand that sped the dart
That pierced the chieftain's breast,
Yet with such witching tenderness
Could tremble in caress!
Dreams of the heart that proudly braved
A nation's deadly hate,
Yet, at a lover's first command,
Would brook a martyr's fate!

Dreams of the hour when Tululah,
Who so bravely saved his life,
Shall desert her baffled kinsman
To become a white man's wife!
Dreams how he would love and prize her,
Shielding her with tenderest care,
Spending time, and life, and fortune
But to grant her lightest prayer.

But his dream is rudely broken,
And his blanched lip loudly calls,
For he hears the well known rumbling
Of this river's awful falls.
Life was sweet, death was so near,
And he so young to die!
No wonder that his trembling lips
Sought mercy from on high.

He bore ten thousand tortures
With every passing breath,
As he lay bound and helpless,
Gliding swiftly on to death.

He raised his clarion voice
Above the deafening roar;
Great heavens! can a human cry
Reach that resounding shore?

"Yes! Yes!" a once familiar voice
Calls loudly from that shore,
And a well known trapper woos time
To life and hope once more!
By an effort, born of hope renewed,
McCray sprang to his feet;
The trapper saw, his lariat flew,
His outstretched hands to greet.

"*Steady!*" the practical huntsman cried;
"Your peril is almost o'er;
Steady, for in a moment
Your foot shall press the shore!"
Then, as he drew the skiff ashore,
He recognized McCray,
But gazed in silent wonder
For late raven locks were grey!

And never, to his dying day,
Would McCray view the place
Where, in suspended agony,
He met death face to face!
He shuddered at an Indian's name,
And soon forgot the Queen,
Who once so bravely saved him
From a nation's senseless spleen.

He wooed and won a maiden
Whose blue eyes, like your own,
Held within their liquid depths,
Love's nectarine full blown,
And as I press your luscious lips
I praise thee, brave McCray,
Whose dauntless courage gave to me
The girl I hold today!

Oh, yes: forgive me, darling,
I did almost forget;
But how can mortal silence keep
By such sweet eyes beset?
Grant me the boon of one more kiss
And gaze into my face;
Light fancy by your radiant eyes,
Tululah's fate to trace!

Still let the pressure of your hand
Chain me in rapture to the earth,
For I must offer thoughts tonight
That ne'er before had birth!
No idle dreamer dares to pierce
The mystery of this stream,
Nor would I dare the bold emprise
Save that your wish I deem

The highest law my loving heart
Can now or ever know,
And 'neath the witchery of your smile
My raptured numbers glow!
My fancy soars on eager wing,
And will, perhaps, at last,
Gladly at your high behest
Unfold the misty past!

Tululah slept till evening shades
Had deepened into night,
And woke, alas! to find herself
Bereft of her brave knight.
Her Indian wit soon taught her
Oguchu was to blame,
And hastily she found him,
Her eyes and cheeks aflame!

"Oguchu knows your mission:
Your paleface lover fled
While Tululah's starlit eyes
Were wandering 'mid the dead.

He is not worthy of your love;
Let my sister choose a mate;
Oguchu's lodge is open,
Will my sister spurn her fate?"

"My paleface lover is a brave!"
Tululah proudly cried;
"*He* never fled from friend or foe.
Oguchu, thou hast lied!
Thy double tongue is poison-tipped,
Thy words a coward's dart,
Before I clasp thy loathsome form
Let panthers rend my heart!

"Speak, coward, speak! where is my brave?
Tululah asks you where;
Speak, lest I summon by a word
The friends of earth and air
To tear your quivering limbs apart,
You lying, treacherous chief.
Speak the truth! you Indian dog,
The night is growing brief!"

The awestruck chief is conquered,
And tells, with bated breath,
Where last he saw him drifting,
Into the jaws of death!
Tululah heard, and wild despair
Hurled reason from her throne.
Low at her feet the wretches crouched,
Their treachery to atone!

"Up! Up, you cowards! Up, you knaves!
And lead me to the place.
Tululah's hand shall save him yet
Or curse your coward race!
'T is mine to speak; yours, to obey;—
I am your Virgin Queen:—
I *swear* to save my lover
Or *nevermore* be seen!"

They led her to the river,
And, pointing to the place,
They stood like criminals abashed
Before the judge's face.
She spurned their pleading counsel,
And, springing in a boat,
She cast the oars from her
And set the skiff afloat!

Then, as she gazed adown the stream,
Her eyes were all aglow
With that deep yearning passion
Such hearts alone can know.
While sitting in the boat erect,
With an Indian's willowy grace,
She sang in tuneful numbers
A song time can't efface:

"I am coming, coming, coming,
    Slowly drifting down the stream,
While my heart is yearning, yearning
    For the idol of love's dream.

"I have left them—left them—left them!
    Farewell, treacherous Indian race;
I can hear him calling, calling,
    And I go to seek his face.

"Now I'm gliding, gliding, gliding!
    And I hear the awful roar
Of the waters tumbling, tumbling,
    Where no boat will need an oar!

"Now I'm rushing, rushing, rushing!
    And the spray obscures my sight;
The angry waters leaping, leaping,
    Chill me with a strange affright.

"Oh, I see him! see him—see him,
    And I welcome death's alarms!
Oh! I'm swiftly falling, falling,
    And I spring into his arms!"

Not a trace of boat or maiden
Could the savage searchers find,
And they fled the spot in terror,
Daring not to look behind!
Nor would they tarry near the river,
But moved their wigwam's far away;
No savage Creek would linger
Near the spot by night and day.

And tradition says her spirit
May be seen on nights like this,
When the heavy moon, mist-laden,
Greets the river with a kiss!
Not in vain will be our vigil
If Tululah knows tonight
In your precious veins is flowing
Genuine blood of her brave knight!

Look! Look! 'mid the river's silvery sheen
Tululah's Phantom Boat is seen,
While the air vibrates like a quivering lyre,
Touched by the hands of an angel Choir!
Oh, wondrous music soft and low,
Like rippling streamlets' gentle flow!
Oh, pathos laden, heart refrain,
No mortal lips can breathe that strain!

Immortal love! not even death
Can damp thy flame or chill thy breath!
Nay, while eternal ages roll,
'T is thine to feed the hungry soul
With manna dipped in passion's fire,
True birthright of the heart's desire;
Blest food no mortal lips can take
And fail enrapturing bliss to wake!

Heaven's corner-stone, earth's chief delight,
Tululah's captive soul tonight
Is but living o'er the dream
Thou didst create beside this stream.

Her hapless fate all must deplore,
Self-sacrificed in days of yore;
And, could Tululah live again,
At least one heart would soothe her pain!

The legend may be overdrawn,
Yet 't is not all a dream!
Nor will you ever say again:
"This is no haunted stream!"
Other eyes beside our own
Have seen the Phantom Boat,
And other ears than ours have heard
That wild, wierd music float!

But, precious little darling,
As I strain thee to my breast,
I am concious you are weary,
Thus deprived of needful rest.
Let us hasten to thy cottage,
Parting with a lingering kiss;
Little Daisy, then, can slumber
And awake in perfect bliss!

AN INITIAL ACROSTIC.

Hear, O hear the melting music pouring from inspired hearts!
In the race of life they stumbled, victims of temptation's darts.
Ruin's billows them engulfing, all their hopes and joys to blight;
And the scorpion lash of conscience scourges them by day and
   night!
Man has doomed them to a prison where shame's torrents hourly
   roll

Pouring every known affliction on the crushed and bleeding soul!
Every legal right has perished, every social tie is snapped!
Crushing Force is ever present, body mind and soul entrapped!
Kindness is a total stranger, human treatment rarely shown.

Man *is* faultless when his fellow for a fault must needs atone!
Can such beings know the rapture Heaven decrees to poet souls?

Know they where to place the cymbals of the sounding lyre
Never yet has human malice stilled the music of the spheres!
In *the loathsome prison dungeon Heaven the sweetest music hears!*
Guilt or shame, or human anger, ne'er can fold the poet's wings.
Howsoever deep his anguish, still his heart exultant sings—
Tunes his lyre, srill triumphant, and to you these pages brings!

ACROSTIC TRIBUTE TO

DR. H. R. PARKER.

BY GEO. W. H. HARRISON.

He towers above his fellow men, like some grand knight of old.
Endeavoring to right all wrong with spirit bold and free!
No craven fear usurps his soul, no task his spirit quails.
Religion to his soul is *love*, and love no wrong entails!
Ye who love eternal right and wish your fellows well

Refuse him not the meed of praise—'t is his our aches to quell!
Each heart within these prison walls that tests his wondrous skill
Unites to sing his praises and bless his generous will.
By kindly words he cheers the soul of those whom dread disease
Envelops in her mystic folds and gives each patient ease.
Taught caring for their praise or blame, he steers his course aright.

Proving duty, well performed, is matchless in its might.
And, tho' but a youth in years, his well instructed mind
Reveals all pathologic truth and practice well combined.
Kindly may the fates decree that he may rise to fame,
Ever free, as he is now, from error and from shame.
Refuse him naught of happiness and bless his honored name!

LINES TO MY WIFE.

BY GEO. W. H. HARRISON.

Years and years have passed away
  Since last we met, my darling wife:
Oft have I felt the tooth of pain
  Gnaw at the vitals of my life.

The brow thy hand has oft caressed
  With such sweet, hypnotic power,
The lines of care and grief has traced
  And wrinkled, like a withered flower.

The dark brown locks you loved so well,
  Now interspersed with silver thread,
Shows plainly that the march of time
  Has left its footprints on my head.

The deep gray eyes that once could flash
  With passion's fire, or melt in love,
Have lost the wanted fires of youth,
  Like some poor offcast, limpsy glove.

Yet in my breast there beats a heart
  That never will nor can grow old;
Thy image keeps its pulses warm
  With love that never shall grow cold.

Thy grace and beauty won that heart
  Long years ago, when thou wert young;
Thy gentle, generous, faithful care
  Has bred a love I cannot tongue.

Heaven can grant no sweeter bliss,
  To crown the evening of my life,
Than lulu's sweet, enraptured kiss,
  When time restores me to my wife.

Out of the Depths.

BY GEO. W. H. HARRISON.

In a cell of rock and iron,
Where remorse and shame environ,
Sat a convict sadly dreaming—
Dreaming of the days of yore,
Dreamed he of a land of flowers
Where, amid Love's smiling bowers,
He had spent such happy hours,
To memory ne'er so sweet before.
And he softly, fondly questioned:
 "Shall I know such bliss once more?"
 Hope made answer, "*Yes, once more!*"
In a home which love had founded,
Now by grief and care surrounded,
Sat a wife and mother, weeping,
 Weeping for her prisoned swain.
Wept she o'er fate's mad endeavor,
That such loving hearts could sever,
With a blow, that seemed to never
Lose its agonizing pain;
And her cry arose to heaven:
 "Father, shall we meet again?"
 Mercy answered, "Once again."
Ope those doors of latticed iron,
Lift the clouds that now environ;
Faithfulness shall be rewarded—
 Love the victory hath won.
Learn that I, your God, am heeding
Prayers that rise from hearts now bleeding,
And my hand is ever leading,
 Tho' the clouds obscure the sun.
Bows my heart in adoration—
 Shall my lips repeat Amen?
 Hope and faith repeat! "Amen."

ELLA REE'S REVENGE.

Beside Saluda's silver stream,
Where flowers nod and poets dream,
A cabin stood, in days gone by,
Whose history should never die.

Here lived and led a blameless life,
Brave Hayward and his peerless wife,
With three sweet pledges of that love,
Cradled on earth, but born above.

Surrounding them, on every hand,
Was the Red man's native land.
No paleface, save themselves, ever dared
To live in wild these Indians shared.

Treacherous alike in peace and war,
The Seminole obeyed no law
Save one he spake with bated breath:
"Traitors shall die a coward's death!"

The haughty chief who led this tribe,
Fear could not daunt nor favor bribe;
And this lone settler, living here,
Knew white man never dared come near.

He Caucanoe's heart had won
By a kindness nobly done,
In rescuing from a watery grave
The favorite child of this fierce brave.

A frail canoe—swamped in mid stream;
A father's cry—a maiden's scream;
A hunter bearing a maid ashore,
A volume writ would tell no more.

"The land beside this murmuring stream
Thy future home, brave paleface, deem,
And on Caucanoe's word depend,
No Indian dares molest my friend!"

"Yours 't was to save Caucanoe's pride,
Mine be it to protect your bride;
If here a future you would seek,
I listen: Let my brother speak."

"Great Chief! your words, so kind and true,
Fall on my ears like evening dew;
Ere the buds begin to swell
Your brother 'mid your tribe shall dwell."

So Hayward built, with eager haste,
As best befits a woman's taste,
A cabin palace, reared by art,
Each room as secret as your heart.

Here they lived and tilled the ground,
The happiest pair for miles around;
The Indians swarmed around their door
With useful gifts to swell their store.

Caucanoe often sought their door
And played with the children, o'er and o'er,
He brought them many a curious toy,
Their happy childhood to employ.

The winsome sprite, who sat on his knee,
Pleased him most of the guileless three;
Her limped eyes and golden hair
Caucanoe thought divinely fair.

As the happy years flew swiftly by,
Beneath Caucanoe's watchful eye,

PRISON POETRY.

Paralee grew, with rapid pace,
Into a maid of faultless grace.

Caucanoe loved this lovely child
With a passion fierce, and deep, and wild,
Yet hopeless, he feared, that love would be,
Since naught could bridge the raging sea

Of racial and tribal pride,
That lay between them, deep and wide;
And well he knew another's soul
Brooked naught on earth save his control.

King Ulca's daughter, the proud Ella Ree,
Graceful and lithe as a willow tree,
With eyes and hair like the raven's wing,
And voice as soft as the babbling spring,

Had sought him for her wigwam brave,
Weeping o'er his late wife's grave;
And well he knew the tears she shed,
By tribal law their bodies wed.

True love for her he could not feel,
Yet such a fact dared not reveal;
His squaw she was alone in name
And never to his wigwam came.

Another love, oh, fateful thought!
With direful misery doubly fraught,
Surged and tossed within his soul
Until it spurned his late control.

At last he sought her much loved side
And begged her to become his bride.
The maiden heard and laughed outright,
And thus let loose the fiends of night

That of late had lain at rest
Within Caucanoe's savage breast.
Now, naught could stay this rising ire
Save to light the Council Fire.

At last among his braves he stood,
Like some monarch of the wood;
While burning words flowed from his tongue.
That showed how deep his heart was wrung.

The Council heard and thus decreed:
"Our land from paleface dogs be freed.
Tomorrow night the proud paleface
Shall rue Caucanoe's late disgrace!"

"'T is well," the haughty chief replied;
"Who scorns to be Caucanoe's bride
Shall feel a living flame of fire
Quench the last spark of life's desire!"

But, ere the morrow's sun had set,
Awakening love brought deep regret.
Love fought the savage till he fell,
And Pity's tears began to well.

He crept the cabin light within,
And there confessed his double sin.
"'T is done," he cried, "you shall not die;
The boat is ready; up, and fly!

"Saluda's stream shall guide you right.
Caucanoe lays to die tonight!
Once you are free, I die content.
Nor deem the blow untimely sent."

The boat has left the silent shore,
And Hayward tugs at the muffled oar;

The craft sweeps on, like a thing of life,
Impelled by the prayers of a weeping wife.

Caucanoe stood on the bank hard by,
With heaving breast and tear-dimmed eye,
That proved a hero's soul could rest
In the natural dome of a savage breast.

The flashing oars in the moonlight pale
Give forth no sound and leave no trail;
Naught is heard save the breath
Of the fleeing ones in their race with death.

Hark! What means that frightful yell?
'T is a cry of triumph, born of hell;
Their savage foe, long under way,
At last have seen their wanted prey.

They see the foe and wildly fly
The flashing oars, till they almost fly;
"We'll yet be saved," brave Hayward spoke.
But his oars shivered beneath his stroke.

He sprang to his feet, with ashen face,
And his trusty rifle flew to its place;
A maddening yell from the savage crew
Proved the ball to the mark had straightway flew.

Six times his trusty rifle spoke;
Each time an Indian skull it broke.
His gallant sons stood near their sire
And reinforced his deadly fire!

Their doom was sealed. The savage horde
Soon reached their bark and sprang aboard;
Yet scorned they even then to yield,
While strength was left a knife to wield.

Each one dared a hero's part;
Each knife it sought a savage heart,
Nor did they cease to bathe in gore
Till they sank beneath to rise no more.

Paralee and her mother lay
To savage hands an early prey;
For neither knew, nor felt they ought,
Of what they did or what they sought,

Since terror and alarm, too deep,
Had locked their senses all in sleep.
Alas! that they should ever wake:
Returning senses meant the stake.

Soon homeward with the living dead
The savage horde in triumph sped;
And bore to haunts of Ella Ree
The paleface foe she longed to see.

Better for Paralee had she died
Amid the battle's raging tide.
"Not wounded tigress in her lair
More dangerous than a jealous fair!"

Assembled around the Council Fire,
With haughty mien and rising ire,
Each chief was ready to relate
His own exploit or vent his hate.

Safely bound by cruel thong,
In the center of the throng,
The captives sat in silent dread.
Envying none except the dead.

"Brothers! the paleface Ella Ree,
Whose words from guile are always free,

Will tell you all you need to know,
Who scorns *her* words must brave my blow!"

Thus Ulca spake, then glared around
With a mighty monarch's haughty frown,
"That held his hearers more in awe
Of his dread prowess than his law."

"Chief! Warriors! Braves in battle tried,
Your blood Saluda's stream has dyed;
Your brothers sleep no more to wake!
Will *you* sit by nor vengeance take?"

"A traitor warned the doomed paleface;
Shall *he* yet live to brave our race?
How the white lily wrought the spell,
Caucanoe, and not I, must tell!"

"Caucanoe does not fear to die!
'T was he that bade the paleface fly;
Let these women now be set free;
Vent your hate alone on me."

"Paralee I loved, and her alone;
Mine was the fault—let me atone.
Ella Ree, herself, shall light the fire
And chant around my funeral pyre."

"Loose the captive! Raise the stake!
It shall be thus," brave Ulca spake.
"If love shall brave the cruel flame,
You captives go from whence they came."

In haste they reared the ready stake,
And bade the Chief his place to take.
He lightly stepped in proper place,
A conquering smile upon his face.

The signal given—a lighted brand—
Ella Ree raised with trembling hand,
Yet begged Caucanoe not to die,
But to her willing arms to fly.

Pardon was his, both full and free,
As the proud brave of Ella Ree;
The hated captives should atone
For all blood spilt, and they alone!

Caucanoe frowned and thus replied:
"If Ella Ree would be my bride,
Let her light the fire and stand
Here beside me, hand in hand."

Forward she sprang—the torch applied,
Even in death a happy bride!
Saluda's stream is never free
From the dying chant of Ella Ree!

THE MURDERER'S DREAM.

Ye glittering stars! how fair ye shine tonight,
And, oh, thou modest moon! thy silvery light
Comes streaming through these iron bars before me.
How clear and silent is this lovely night!
How quiet and how bright!
I nothing hear, nor aught can hear
Me when I speak, but stone and iron that I fear;
I, shunned by all, as if alone I'd go to Hell;
I, alone in chains! Ah, me, the cruel spell
That brought me here. Heaven could not cheer me
Within these cursed walls—within this dark and dreary cell.
This gloomy, cold, and solitary Hell.

And thou, O Time! the only thing that's not my foe—
O Time! O Time! thou passeth on so slow,
Keeping my soul in terror, in bondage, and in woe;
Was I to blame? I was, they say; they say 't is so.
Oh, God! will this deep crimson, aye, black stain
My nervous system always strain!
Will my foul crime forever haunt my brain?
Must I live here in earthly fear, and never, never hear
The sweetest voice to me of all, I've heard not for a year?
Must I this torture feel, year after year?
Live, die in Hell, and yet a Paradise so near?
Wilt Thou, Oh, God! wilt Thou not hear? "T is I, 't is I they all
    do fear.

Am I to Thee, O Christ, as dead? Thou who sought
The lonely prisoner in his dismal cell, and to him taught
The true and only law to govern man—Thy love,
Which can be only reached by prayer to Thee above?
In this cold and darkened cell, dost Thou reprove
My soul? Dost Thou doom it to endless misery?
Am I so wicked, sinful, that I cannot move
Thy loving kindness, to a slight reprove?
Ah, me, ah, me, 't is love Thou sayest—love,
Canst I at this late day by full repentence see
The divine, the holy, ever cleansing love in Thee?
Canst Thou be Christ and have no love for me?

What, can it be that I am lost and 'll never know thy bliss?
And for my cruel, wicked crime no joy above all this?
What, world of sin! What, never? Is my destiny Hell?
Is that my cruel sentence because in sin I fell?
Aye, I did fall! Into that dark and fathomless pit,
And now in Hell my soul has fell, and for Hell it is not fit;
Into that misery eternal, where nothing lives but all 's infernal
Is there my future — is it there?
My thoughts they burn my head, my heart 't was, ah, 't was dead
But now it lives, and in my breast does burn:
Those pains, and, severe as they were, they flew, yes, flew away,
And being absent for awhile, remorse came in by day.

Oh, God, Oh, God, I am not fit for this infernal Hell!
Oh, mercy, mercy! my destiny, 't is here that I must dwell.
Away! away! ye fiery fiends, I am among you now,
O Christ, O Savior of the sinner! To Satan must I bow?
Pray, take me back to earth again, and test me one and all,
And let me live anew my life and see if I will fall.
Test me, test me once again, let me hear the old church bell,
'Cause now I 'm so much steeped in sin that I 'm not fit for Hell.
Oh, horrors! horrors! hear the groans of tortured victims there,
Some young, and many are quite old, I know it by their hair!
Poor, poor, poor wretches, see them there, all bleeding and in chains;
I know they realize their fate, because they all have brains.

Is this the horrid, horrid place my mother taught was Hell?
Oh, see those brutal fiery fiends, they call them "Imps" you know,
And many an one has feared them here, because of sin he'd sown.
Just see the demons of the deep! Just hear their hellish tones!
Then floating back on brimstone air comes mocking, mocking groans.
See, see the devils how they dance, with brimstone torches how they prance;
What! can it be they look like men and 'stead of hearts they have but sin
And grinning hang around me? Oh, fearful, fearful fire of hell, what can it be within?
They sneer and stare at me! Go 'way, ye devils cooked in sin and crime!

I 'm now in Purgatory waiting for the time
When by the law of a just God I 'll be removed from here,
And by the law of Christ divine, of thee I 'll have no fear.

Hark! List! From yonder corner comes loud cries,
Oh, let me hold my aching, bursting head!
They come from some poor wretch that dies,
And many an one may mourn him now as dead.
I see him! I see him! There he is! My murdered victim now
Appears before me. That is him! and to him I must bow.
Oh, his cries, his groans, they haunt me
To the bottom of my wicked heart. Can it be
That I must dwell forever in this wretched misery?
Horrors! See him now reach out his bony hand
To grasp me firmly by the throat and hold me like a band.
Take me, demons, if you please, take me into Hell!
Anything you choose may do—remove me from this cell!

My soul, my soul, awake! awake! They come! they come!
The devil's come to take—Old Satan, I am thine!
Away my soul will ever roll through torturing, scorching Hell,
And down into the blackest depths my soul is cast pell-mell.
Oh, what a fate for man to meet—speak, Satan! speak, I say!
And with your torturing, devilish deeds—my ruin! no delay!
What dumb! Old Satan, canst thou speak? Look here
And speak thy want! I 'm now right crisp and hard in sin and
    haven't any fear.
Take me, demons! Take me, quick! I hear the awful knell
Of the roaring, moaning billows, and the bitterness of Hell.
Take me, Satan, take me! as my fate is firmly sealed,
While ye in Hades do wake me, and o'er me the batoon wield.

What! What! Am I mistaken? Was it only but a dream?
I, still living here on earth—oh, how real it all did seem.
Could I now just one chance have and in mercy be forgiven,
I would have respect for all and send prayers right up to heaven.
When on earth Christ did come to save sinners from their fate,
Any time they 'd turn to Him they 'd find 't was not too late.
Holy Savior, heavenly dove, Thou who reigns supreme above!
Though in sin I have been dead, I am saved just by Thy love.

Could I only have good sight, that I could see my sad plight,
I would always to Thee cling, and to Thee cling with my might.
Now, to Thee let me give thanks, 'cause 't was only a bad dream,
But its horrors to me cling, 'cause so real it all did seem.

ACROSTIC TRIBUTE TO

GOD'S MESSENGERS.

CHAPLAIN AND MRS. C. L. WINGET.

Cyprian, the father of the orators' plan, a preacher, a priest and godly man;
You have been, by the good Lord sent, on the mission your heart is ever bent.
Passed through trials of life severe, God was good when He sent you here,
Right in the midst of a sweltering gang of sinners, corrupt on every hand.
I, for one, have watched you keen, and from you haven't an evil deed seen;
All has been so easy to see that your whole soul's bent on setting us free—
Not from earthly, bodily pains, but from our evil, and sin, and shame!

Lee was the second choice of name, she christened her son for Heavenly fame.
Each and every day she taught him ever sin to brave, till dear mother she went down into an early grave.
Every day and every hour he tries to keep that august dower, and meet her where there's endless time, in Heaven's pure and holy clime.

Winget came unto this place to save poor sinners by God's own grace;
An eloquence and heartfelt plea he's prayed for us on bended knee;
Nor has his pleading been in vain, because from us he's driven pain.
"God help the prisoner!" is his prayer, while lingering in this prison lair;
"Eternal justice may they have while life's hard struggle they do brave!"
"To God be praise! we see His face. God save the prisoner by Thy grace!"

Susan, his wife and better half, and one of God's own kind,
Upon each bright and sabbath morn she helps the text to find.
She 's ever there, in the arm chair, through service and through song,
And with kindly smile she does beguile the prisoners from all wrong.
May—let us bow unto you now, thou noble, holy one, and may God speed for all your need for the good that you have done.

Gregory is an ancient name, to you it has been given:
Right down deep in your friendly heart is found the truth of Heaven
Each of us prisoners here confined for truth will e'er contend:
Go, search each heart! and then report if truth we 'll not defend.
Onward, onward, upward, upward may your labors ever roll;
Reach out for poor fallen sinner, and your work we 'll all extol;
Yet 't is not too late to labor—God will answer, "Aye, extol!"

"Fair-child" of Heaven's august plan, how comest thou to wed yourself to Man?
A name is nothing but to designate, but, Oh—how often it does consecrate
In language pure and clear as diamond scale, while thou, Fair-child, we, every one, do hail!
Real sympathy is not so strong a band as binds fair woman unto haughty man!
Come, hasten! now thy work be done, 'cause life's short race is almost run!
He whom thou wed so many years ago has been God's servant faithfully to do
In words so full of just and holy writ, that in our chapel we do love to sit.
Love for your duty, kind to all you meet, faithful to your Master's cause and a smile for all you greet.
Do by us as you have done and never do complain, because the work that you have done has not been done in vain!

"Winget" is the name you chose to support the once Fair-child.

In christian mission go forth God's castles for to build;
Never forget the prisoner close locked in dungeon cell.
Go forth and teach to him The Life of the soul you love so well.
Each hour you spend in christian work is never thrown away.
The Truth is known! you'll harvests reap in Heaven's golden day!

THE MIND IS THE STANDARD OF THE MAN.

In chains and shackles closely bound;
  They say I am a prisoner;
Although in this small cell I 'm found,
  A prisoner I am not.
The door is made of iron bars,
  The lock is large and strong,
But my mind soars free, up to the stars,
  As if I 'd done no wrong.
The mind of man is ever free,
  By nature's law itself,
While this wicked, wretched corpus
  May be laid upon the shelf.
What of this wretched body?
  What care we for this hand?
But there 's one thing safe to wager on,
"THAT MIND 'S THE STANDARD OF THE MAN."

They may chain me fast unto the rock,
  And bind both hands and feet;
They may keep me far off in the dark,
  Where friends I cannot meet;
They may call me vile and wicked wretch,
  And murderer and thief;
They may say I am an infidel
  And steeped in unbelief;
They may say I 'm false and awful bad,
  And lend not a helping hand;
They may sow the seed North, East, South, West,
  Far, far throughout the land;
They may go right on with falsity

And it publish like a ban.
But there 's one thing safe to wager on,
"THAT MIND 'S THE STANDARD OF THE MAN."

If the mind was easy to be read,
  And another for to see,
There would prisoner after prisoner
  Immediately be set free.
If conscience was as easy known
  As another's words to hear,
There would not be half so many men
  That society would fear.
But what do people think or care
  What 's in another's brain,
So long as *they* can all conceal
  The evil in *their* frame.
There are a few who secretly
  Do not conceal their sham,
But there 's one thing safe to wager on,
"THAT MIND 'S THE STANDARD OF THE MAN."

If every one was now compelled
  To show life in *true* attire,
They 'd cause the picture to be marred
  And cast into the fire.
They 'd blush with shame to bring to light
  Black spots upon their life;
They kick, and squirm, and twist about,
  And fight it with a strife.
Where is the man on this vile earth
  But what has done some wrong,
And in his mind 's concealed it,
  Tho' it stings him like a thong?
There ne'er was one except the Christ
  Who 'd be perfect in the land!
But there's one thing safe to wager on,
"THAT MIND 'S THE STANDARD OF THE MAN."

What if all conscience could be searched
  Clear through with cathode rays,
How many would cheerfully submit,

Who 'd reached their manhood days?
It might not be the blackest crime
   Known to the criminal code,
But can it be sufficiently white
   To call it very good?
It may not be so good nor bad,
   Nor bad nor good indeed,
But is it plenty good enough
   As a standard for a creed?
You may keep it hid in an air-tight box,
   With psychological band,
Then, you see, 'tis safe to wager
   "That mind 's the Standard of the Man."

So long as minds cannot be seen
   And pictured to the folk,
So long there 'll be deceitfulness
   Played by the earthly crook.
The modern shylock now, who craves
   The sentence of the court,
Is just the man who, many times,
   Society he has hurt.
He stands aloof from other folk,
   And cries with a loud voice:
"Down, down, with evil and all crime!
   Arise, my friends, rejoice!"
But turn on him the cathode rays
   And search him, if you can,
You 'll be convinced, beyond a doubt,
   "That mind 's the standard of the Man."

There 's many a man who 's been misjudged,
   And met his doom and fate;
And the truth thereof could ne'er be learned
   Until it was too late.
If cathode rays could have been used,
   And falsehood put to flight,
There 's many a false and trumped up charge
   Would be knocked clear out of sight.
If the mind of man could only be,
   With this mysterious light,
Just brought out plain on canvas,

In colors clear and bright,
It would spread the truth both far and near,
   Just like a marriage ban,
That the rule ordained by nature is
   "THAT MIND'S THE STANDARD OF THE MAN."

Now, when with cathode rays supplied,
   You start out for a search,
Just drop around some Sabbath morn
   And peep into a church.
If one bald deacon, on his breast,
   Wears a diamond bright and clear,
Just shoot cathode across his pate
   And see what's buried there.
Then up into the pulpit,
   Where the priest all devils dare,
And dart the rays around, about,
   And see what's buried there.
Then to the courtroom wend your way,
   To where the judges ran,
Then bet your bottom dollar
   "THAT MIND'S THE STANDARD OF THE MAN."

Then down into our Congress halls
   Make a dash both bold and free,
And shoot cathode right through them all
   And see what you can see.
Then back into the halls of State,
   And catch them, one and all,
And learn yourself, beyond a doubt,
   How many are there to fall.
Don't be surprised if now you find
   Most foul and blackened crimes,
Because they 're plotting for the gold,
   No matter what the times.
Try and discover, then and there,
   The gold bonds, if you can,
And remember, what is true as truth,
   "THAT MIND'S THE STANDARD OF THE MAN."

Then, when you 're done with the outside world,
   And all of Congress halls,

Return to me and take a walk
  Within these dismal walls,
I'll show you men who represent
  Each county in this State;
They're all accused of crime, you know,
  And sentenced to their fate.
But don't be hasty now to judge
  These men you see about;
Fire cathode rays right through their skulls
  And you may find a doubt.
Courts, lawyers and prejudiced jurors
  Will con-vict if they can,
But there's one thing safe to wager on,
  "THAT MIND'S THE STANDARD OF THE MAN."

In here you'll find there's many a mind
  As free from sin and crime
As congressmen and senators
  Who've been there a long time.
Some of these men in here, you see,
  They got a little tight,
And broke into a chicken coop,
  Because 't was in the night.
Some men you see as you walk with me
  Down through these halls so dreary,
Have, on bended knee, prayed to be free
  Until life's become weary.
They have no money, neither friends,
  Because they're far behind the van,
But still 't is safe to wager
  "THAT MIND'S THE STANDARD OF THE MAN."

And now because my enemies
  Have chained me tight and fast,
And cruel, heartless, brutal curs
  Would hold me to the last—
Look here! I'll freely now submit,
  Turn on your cathode rays
And learn, if now 't is not too late,
  The evil of my ways.
Then go up to that old bribed judge,

And prosecutor, too,
And bring their conscience here by mine
And search all through and through.
Look sharp! And now compare their minds
With this one, if you can.
And then apply the golden rule.
"That mind 's the standard of the Man."

Oh, men of science! if you can
Employ the cathode rays
To take the place of jurymen
In these our latter days;
Let not a man upon the bench
To judge another's fate,
Until to cathode he 's been sent
To search beneath his pate!
If then you see his mind is free
From prejudice and crime,
And he 'll give us all fair justice,
Let him sit there all the time!
But if, upon the other hand,
He won't, although he can,
Then cut him out with the golden rule:
"That mind 's the standard of the Man."

How can you, then, a prisoner make,
When his Mind 's as free as space?
You may chain his feet, and hands, and neck,
And tightly bind his face.
Do what you please, and as you please,
You cannot help but see—
That man is man, where e'er he be,
Because his mind is free!
His mind may roam back to his home,
You cannot tie it down,
And folk may look, and scoff, and scowl,
And always wear a frown.
But when of him they a prisoner make,
The mind they never can,
'Cause God ordained the Golden Rule,
"That mind 's the standard of the Man."

CELL THOUGHTS.

BY GEO. W. H. HARRISON.

In the headlong rush for the Land of Fame
How many are wrecked on the Isle of Shame.
How few heads wear a glittering crown
In the far-away realm of great renown.
'Mid the crowded ranks of the legion of greed
How many are crushed 'neath the wheels of need!

How few ever feel the dainty caress
Of the lingering hand of great success!
In the mad pursuit of the god of gold
What brains are wrecked, what hearts grow cold!
How many will spend their latest day
'Mid the hurtling waters of Poverty Bay!

How many are lured by a siren chime
To a double death in the land of Crime!
How few escape, unscarred, within
The winding walks of the maze of sin!
How many that towered above the stars
Now pine and languish behind the bars!

What a trail of woe a single mistake
Across the page of a life can make!
O, shipwrecked sailor, fix your eye
On the Star of Hope in yonder sky;
Mercy's hand will bring release
And safely lead to the Land of Peace.

THE AUTHOR'S FAREWELL.

Gentle reader, this small volume clearly proves that modern man
Can control his erring brothers with a clear enlightened plan.
Ne'er till now have prison printers voiced, unchanged, a convict's
  tho't!
Is the change with retrogression or with onward progress fraught?
Will this volume change your custom or relieve our horrid pain?
Or shall truth be crushed and bleeding, ever bound in prison
  chain?
Will you cast your glances backward, gathering age along by age,
Proof that man is wholly brutal when controlled by maddening
  rage?
View the pen of downy feathers, where men choked and choked
  to death,
Without power to ask for pardon with their last expiring breath!
See your brother in that river, safely chained to yonder rock,
While his thirst is wildly raging and the waves his tortures mock!
See yon dungeon, dark and dreary, built by human art and skill,
Whose dread mission is to madden any one the *law* says kill!
Visit to the hapless culprit, as in Pagan jail he lies;
See the jailer pass the hemlock, which he quaffs, and then he
  dies!
Think of club, of sword and pistol, of the bloody guillotine:
Of the whipcord, knout and gallows of the noted Wolverine:
Of starvation, rack and torture, of the lash and fiery stake,
And then tell me frankly, reader, did these wrongs one virtue
  wake?

Tell me frankly, honest reader, can two wrongs create a right?
And is man's inhuman conduct pleasing in Jehovah's sight?
Or do pitying angels shudder, as the cruel lash you ply,
Wondering man can be so brutal and the laws of God defy?
Does not conscience loudly thunder: "Sin is but the fruit of hate,
And who stones a helpless brother most deserves that victim's
  fate?
Can abuse and brutal treatment purge the sinner of his guilt?
If so, *come*, within my bosom sheath your dagger to the hilt!
Strike, till every erring mortal at your hands has met his fate,
Then sit down and calmly ponder on your awful lonely state!

You, perhaps, have been quite *faultless;* you, perhaps, no *wrong*
    have done,
If 't is *true,* my peerless brother, *you 're alone beneath the sun!*

Do but think! we once were spotless as the babe on mother's knee!
Trace the causes of our downfall with a mind from malice free,
See, on every licensed corner, fiends incarnate hourly sell
Fiery waters of *damnation,* that create *a living hell!*
Women, once as pure as angels, leading heartless lives of shame;
For the trumpery of fashion dealing off both home and name!
Hear men laud the wealthy scoundrel and attempt to clear his
    ways,
While the poor and honest toiler *none* with pride or pleasure
    pays!
See Religion don the garments of all worldly pride and lust,
While the Savior's honest followers are but trampled in the dust!
See the press, with startling headlines, every vice and sin por-
    tray
That can sink your moral standard or lead innocence astray!
View the legions of temptation strewn along the path of youth,
See how few do practice virtue, and how few *adore* the truth!
There! the cause of crime is patent, and our downfall you behold,
To condemn it in a sentence: "*It was women, wine and gold!*"

If you read this book with caution, you have read *between the
    lines,*
Learning much the careless reader and the critic ne'er divines!
You have seen the author's purpose was to tell the simple truth,
As a tribute to the prisoner and a warning to our youth.
You have seen mistakes and errors that less haste would quickly
    mend,
Yet, with all its imperfections, it may prove a useful friend.
And in future I may publish one with less of hasty thought
That may be— God knows the future—with undying issues fraught.
All tried means have proved abortive yet, my friend, there is a
    plan
That *will* lift each erring brother *to the standard of a man!*
If I can but live to publish what I *know* and long to tell,
You *will* read it and believe it; so, dear reader, *fare-the-well!*

CONCLUSION.

Go, little book, thy destined course pursue!
Collect memorials of the just and true;
And beg of every one who comes thou near
Some token of their friendship and good cheer.
And if by chance some true friends thou should find,
Attach them to thee with both soul and mind;
And if they prove good, faithful friends and true.
To them thou sticketh, as if they loved you--
       Adieu! Adieu!

www.ingramcontent.com/pod-product-compliance
Lightning Source LLC
Chambersburg PA
CBHW032129160426
43197CB00008B/575